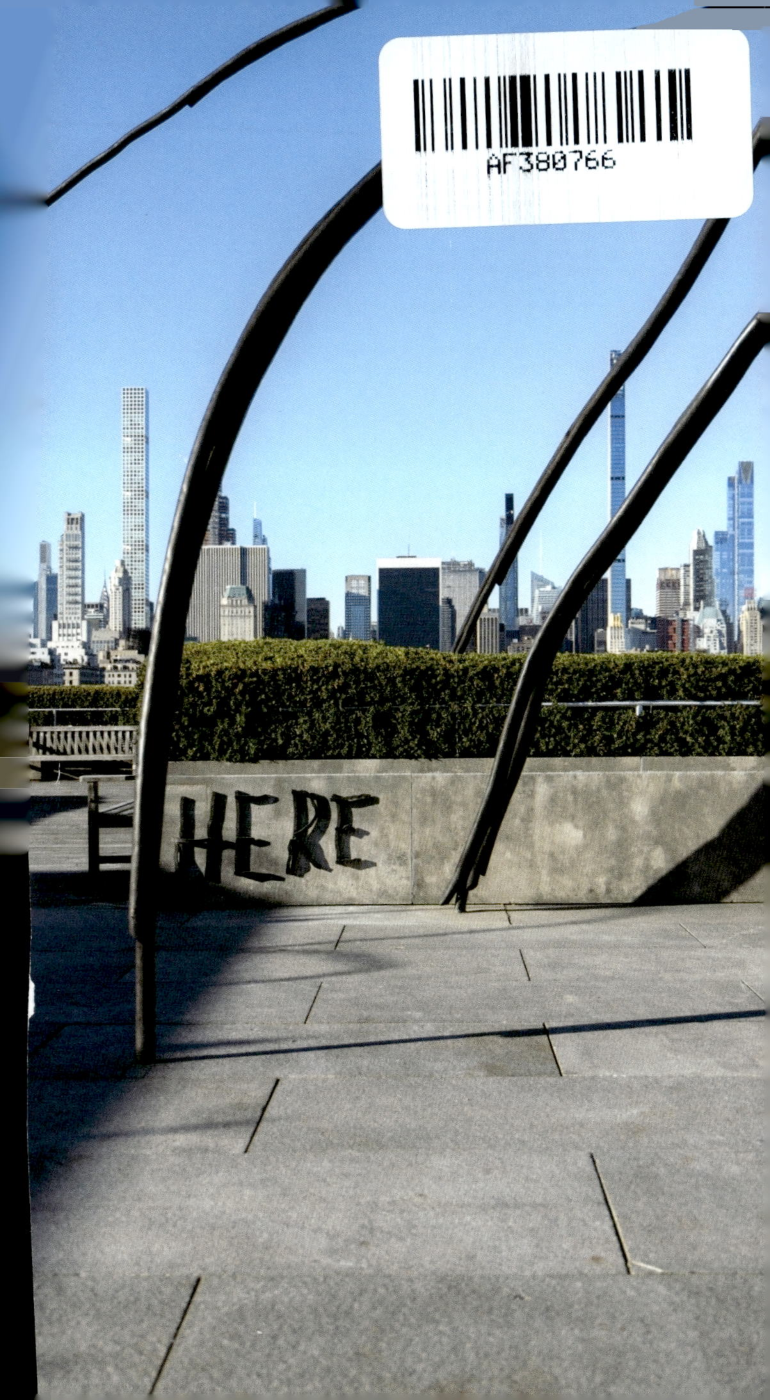
AF380766
HERE

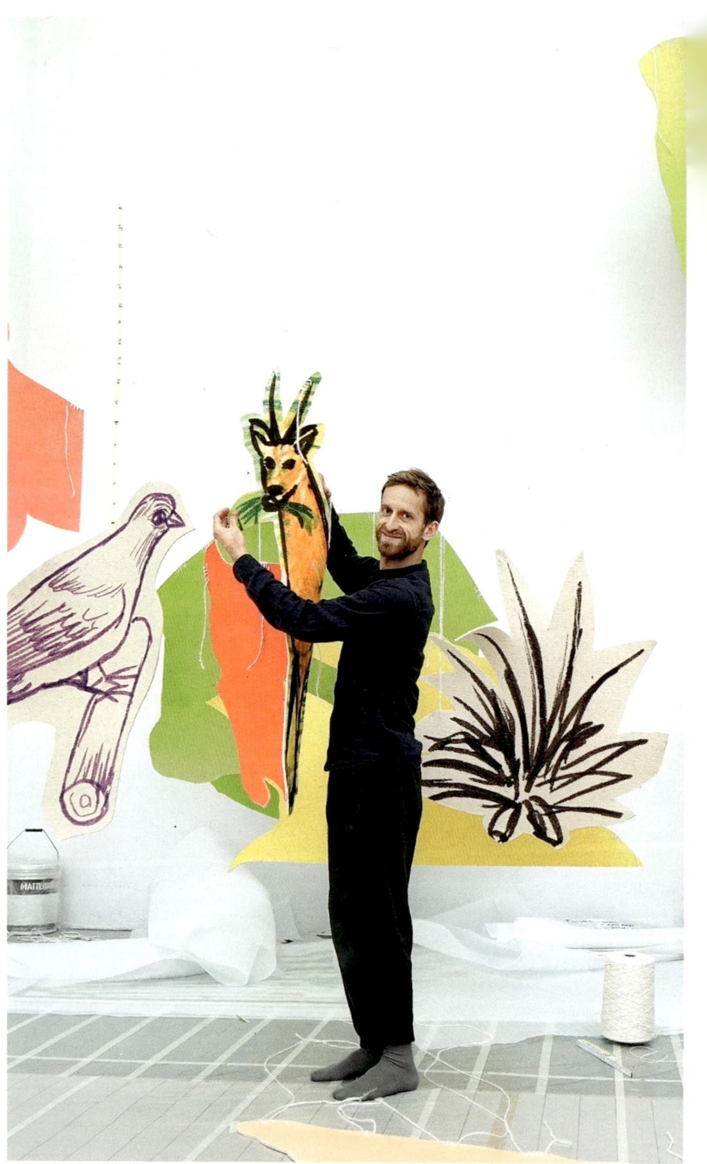

The Roof Garden Commission

Petrit Halilaj
Abetare

David Breslin

Iria Candela

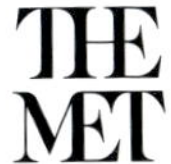

The Metropolitan Museum of Art, New York

Distributed by Yale University Press
New Haven and London

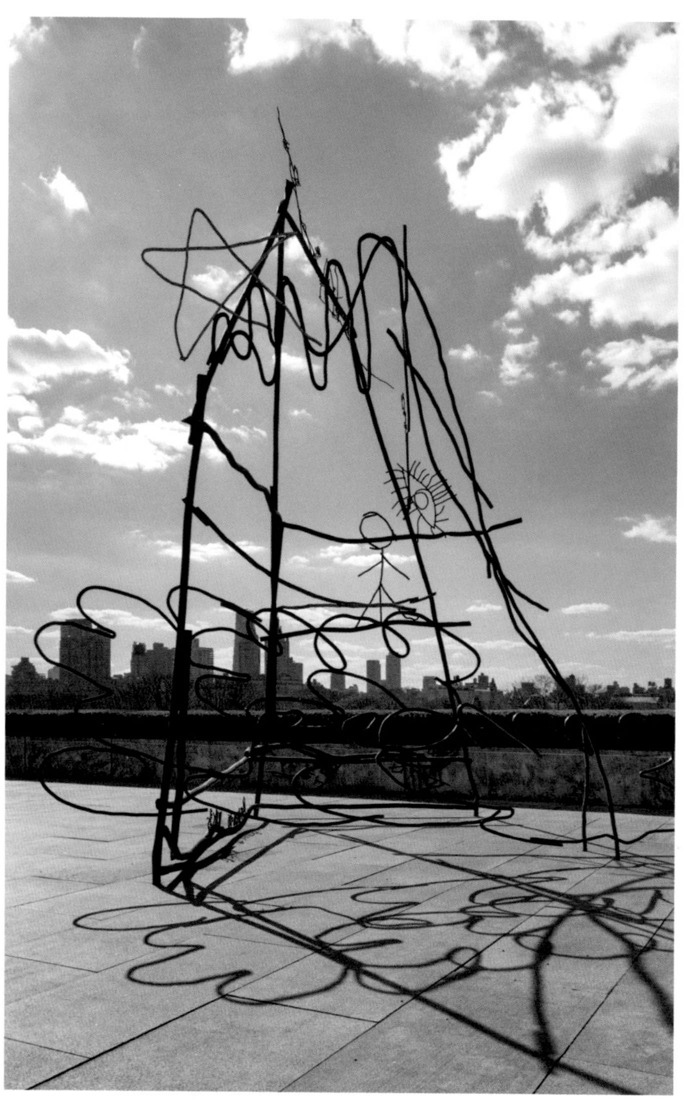

This project is dedicated to all the children whose lives have been interrupted and deeply scarred by wars around the globe. I hope their dreams will fly us to a better future.

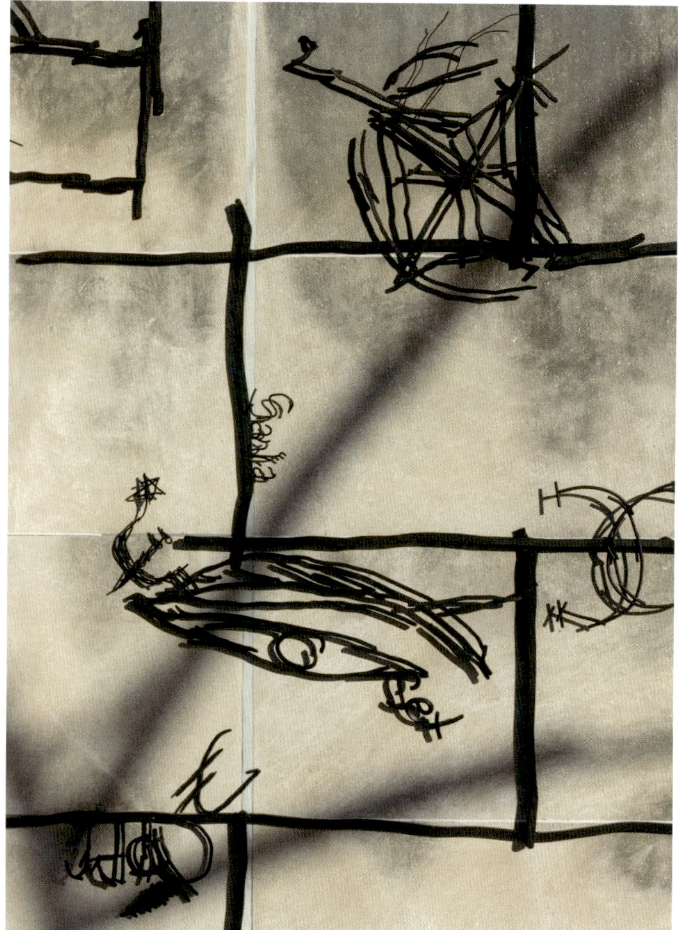

Sponsor's Statement

 with The Metropolitan Museum of Art in support of *The Roof Garden Commission: Petrit Halilaj, Abetare*. For more than fifteen years, we've sponsored exceptional contemporary art exhibitions on The Iris and B. Gerald Cantor Roof Garden, and our commitment continues with Halilaj's sprawling sculptural installation, the artist's first major project in the United States. Halilaj's work draws on his childhood experiences amid conflict in Kosovo while also exploring broader issues of identity, displacement, and personal and global histories.

Bloomberg Philanthropies invests in 700 cities and 150 countries around the world to ensure better, longer lives for the greatest number of people. The organization focuses on five key areas for creating lasting change: the arts, education, environment, government innovation, and public health. The arts are a valuable way to engage citizens and strengthen communities. Through innovative partnerships and bold approaches, the Bloomberg Philanthropies Arts program supports increased access to culture through new technologies and empowers artists and cultural organizations to enhance the quality of life in cities.

**Bloomberg
Philanthropies**

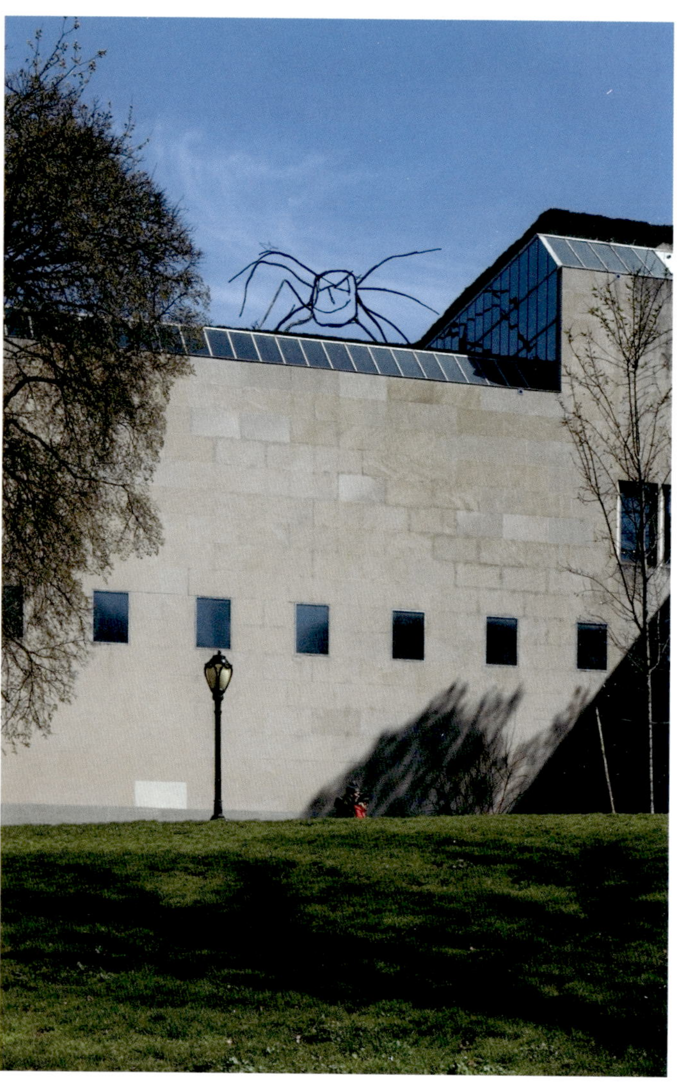

Director's Foreword

Situated atop The Met and surrounded by the Manhattan skyline, The Iris and B. Gerald Cantor Roof Garden has provided unparalleled inspiration to artists invited to create site-specific commissions for this setting.

This year, we are delighted to present an engaging sculptural installation by Petrit Halilaj. Rooted in his homeland of Kosovo, Halilaj's project draws on the collective memory of generations of children in the Balkans, a region whose recent history is marked by traumatic conflicts and territorial divisions. Reconceiving doodles, drawings, and scribbles found on school desks as three-dimensional sculptures set in dialogue with the cityscape, the artist invites us to reconsider the complexity of the childhood imagination and its role in our understanding of contemporary events, whether close to home or far away.

Halilaj's work joins a distinguished group of annual commissions for this site. I would like to thank Iria Candela, Estrellita B. Brodsky Curator of Latin American Art, Department of Modern and Contemporary Art, for curating this year's commission, as well as David Breslin, Leonard A. Lauder Curator in Charge, Department of Modern and Contemporary Art, and the entire Met team for their dedicated work in making it happen.

For its long-standing and generous sponsorship of this commission series, I thank Bloomberg Philanthropies. I am also grateful to Cynthia Hazen Polsky and Leon B. Polsky for their continued support, and to the Diane W. and James E. Burke Fund and the Edward John & Patricia Rosenwald Foundation for meaningful funding for the commission. This catalogue is made possible by the Mary and Louis S. Myers Foundation Endowment Fund.

Max Hollein
Marina Kellen French Director and Chief Executive Officer
The Metropolitan Museum of Art

Some Secret Place of Memory

David Breslin

, a child's scrawled spider perches, giantlike, atop the Iris and B. Gerald Cantor Roof Garden this year. But what home is it making? What trap has been set? Who is it? Petrit Halilaj, speaking as if the bronze and steel sculptures that populate the roof were his children, does not say outright that the spider is his favorite among the brood. Yet, like any parent feigning impartiality, the frequency and ardency with which he refers to it gives him away. He describes the sculpture, with puckish delight, as "my Bourgeois"—a reference to perhaps the most famous spider in art history, Louise Bourgeois's *Maman* (fig. 1), a massive metal arachnid realized by the late French American artist in the 1990s. She had spent decades employing the motif in drawings and smaller sculptures as a stand-in for her mother. As an emblem of maternity, the spider might suggest a being that is protector and predator, a fraught and contradictory psychic territory. Halilaj's genial appropriation does not insist that a viewer know this reference to be moved by the work. It can be experienced just as easily as a manifestation of fear or a materialization of farce. Even so, given the reference he's conjuring, the associative web that centers the mother might begin to catch other connotations, like the motherland, the nation-state, or nationalism itself—the subtext for much of Halilaj's work. Always there, protector and predator, nationalism is so omnipresent that it risks slipping from visibility, awareness, and accountability. And in order for danger to be addressed, of course, it first needs to be seen. This is Halilaj's territory.

When I arrived at his Berlin studio on a warm July afternoon, Halilaj had the preparations for lunch assembled in the courtyard. We caught up as he stoked a small fire where he would later grill vegetables, his eyes flickering restlessly as he described the directions he imagined for this Met commission. Halilaj, at a boyish-looking thirty-seven, has long made childhood a central aspect of his artistic practice. His own life story both compels and complicates this preoccupation— and has also perhaps overdetermined the critical interpretation of his work. His childhood now reads like a myth: displaced from his home in 1998–99 by the war in Kosovo, where ethnic Albanians like Halilaj were subjected to a systematic campaign of terror by Serbian troops, he was temporarily sheltered at a refugee camp in Albania. Artistically

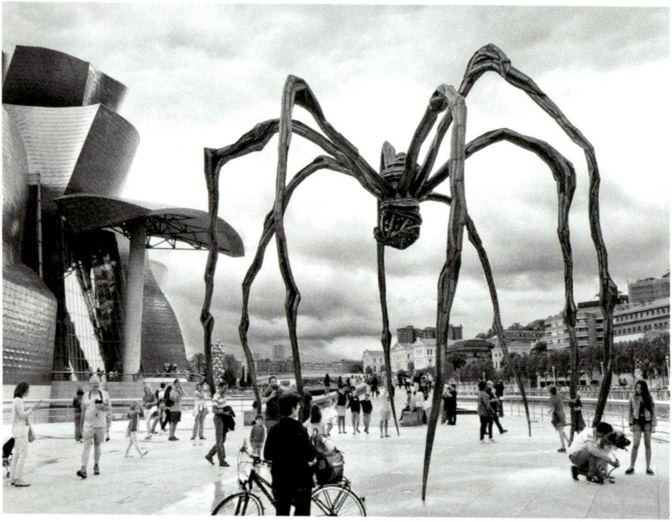

Fig. 1. **Louise Bourgeois**, *Maman*, 1999, cast 2001. Bronze, marble, and stainless steel, 29 ft. 4 ⅜ in. × 32 ft. 1 ⅞ in. × 38 ft. ⅝ in. (895 × 980 × 1160 cm). Installation view at Guggenheim Museum Bilbao

Fig. 2. **Petrit Halilaj** and **Giacomo Poli**, Kukës II, Albania, April 1999. Courtesy of Giacomo Poli

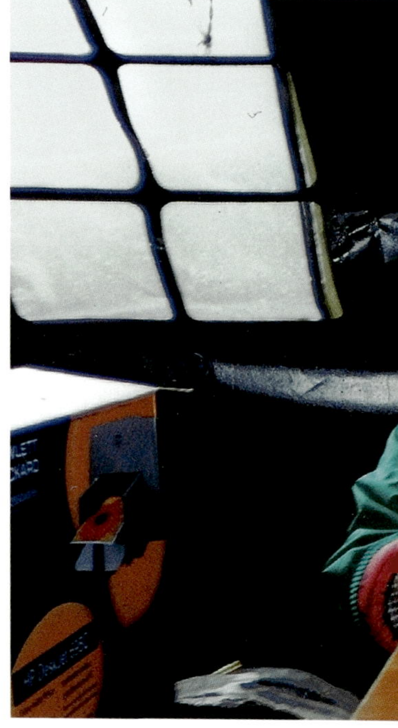

precocious and camera-friendly, he was documented at the Kukës II refugee camp showing his drawing of a massacre to Kofi Annan, then secretary-general of the United Nations (UN). An Italian psychologist named Giacomo Poli, whom Halilaj now describes as like a second father, had encouraged the children in the camp to draw as a differently mediated, nonverbal path toward contending with the brutality they had witnessed (fig. 2). While many of the drawings Halilaj made there refer to specific incidents, such as the Račak massacre of January 1999, others depict peaceful idylls, birds of paradise, and sites of fantasy. This blend of fact and fabulation conspires to provide a visual reckoning of the desire to survive—and how the human consciousness toggles between reality and projection to arrive at a hoped-for future. For a recent project at Tate St Ives (fig. 3), Halilaj used those childhood drawings as starting points, presenting them cut, collaged, and scaled up into a traversable landscape of nightmares and daydreams. As we spoke on that summer day, I watched Halilaj grow so animated about an idea that he bounded from his seat and skipped (literally) into the studio to retrieve some papers he wished to share. I immediately

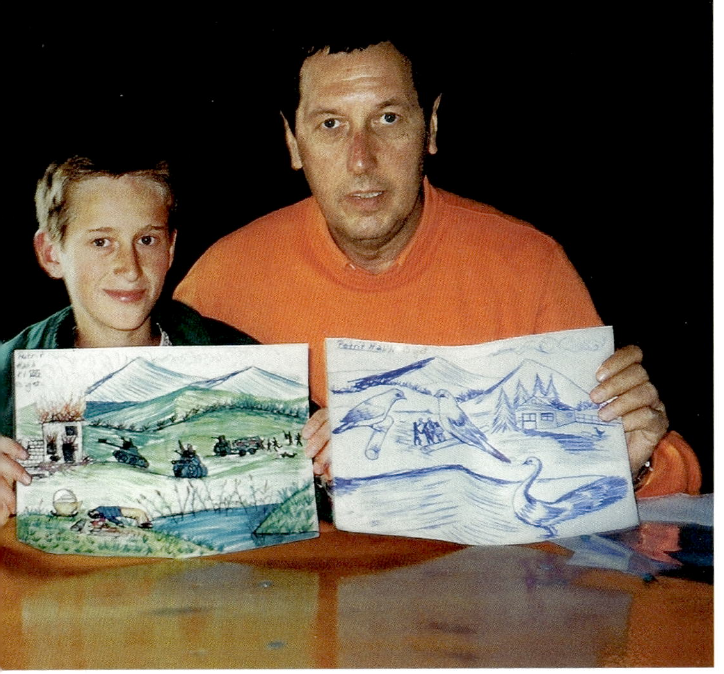

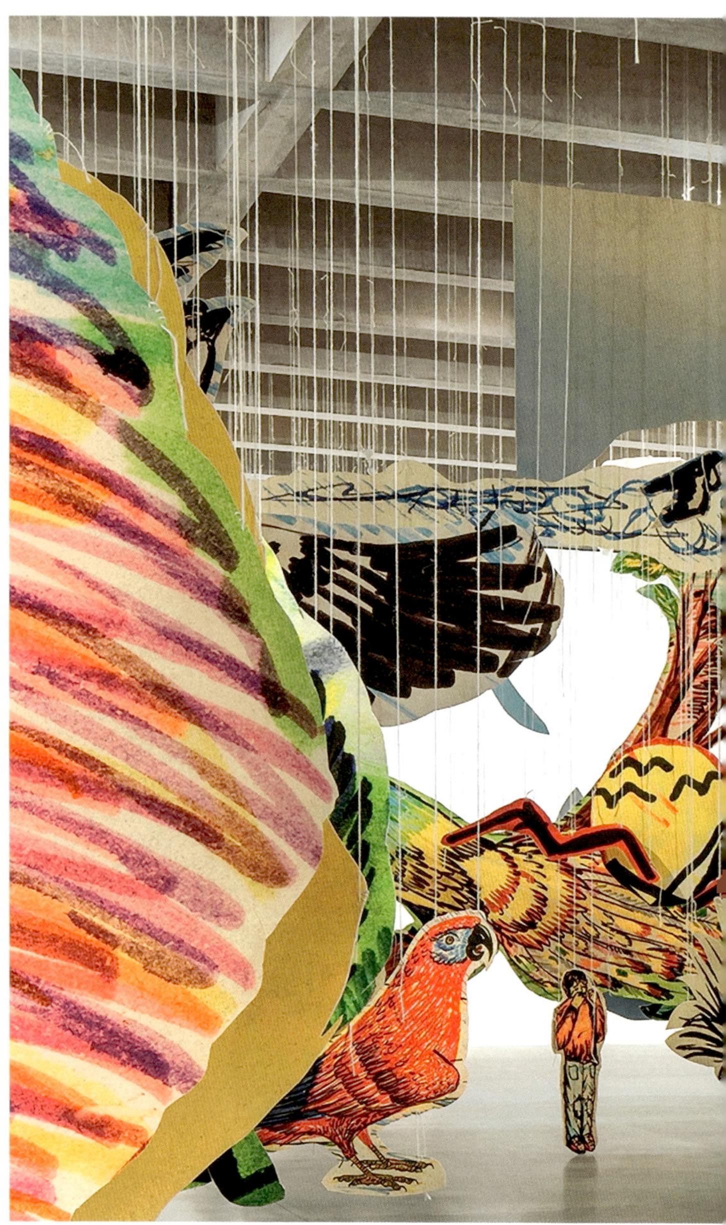

Fig. 3. **Petrit Halilaj**, *Very volcanic over this green feather*, 2021. Installation view at Tate St Ives, Cornwall, United Kingdom

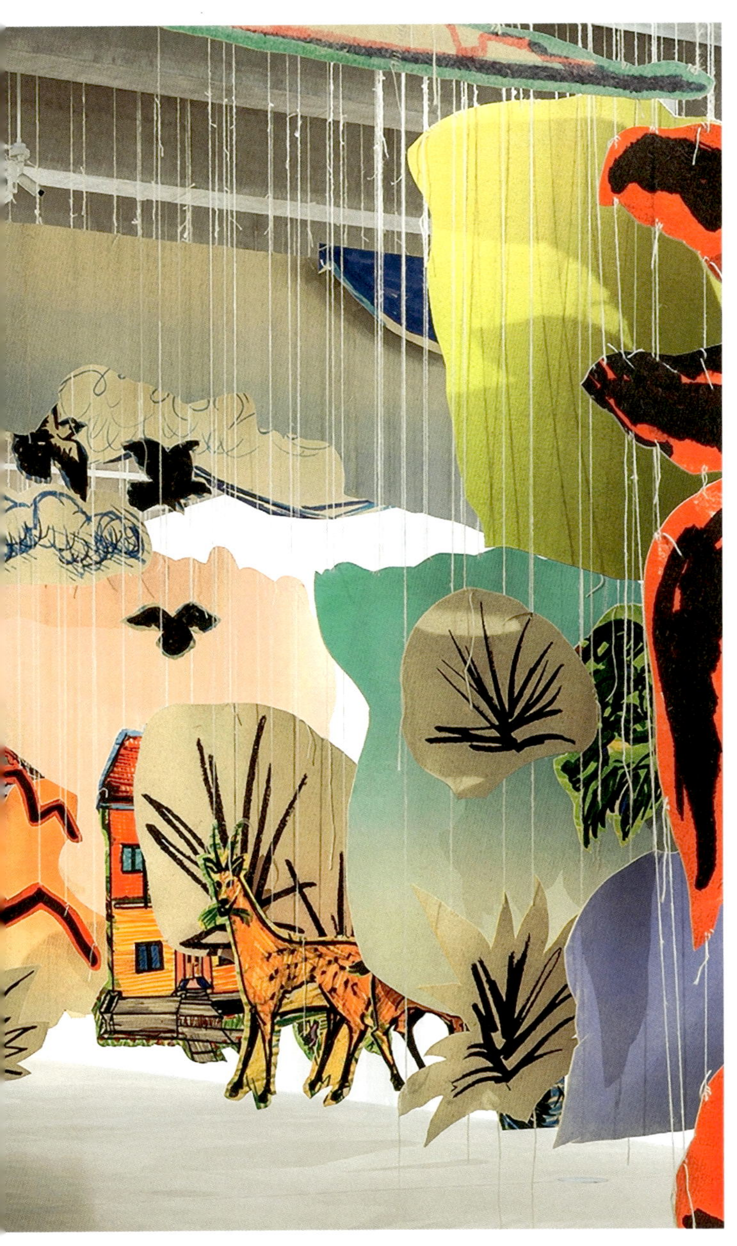

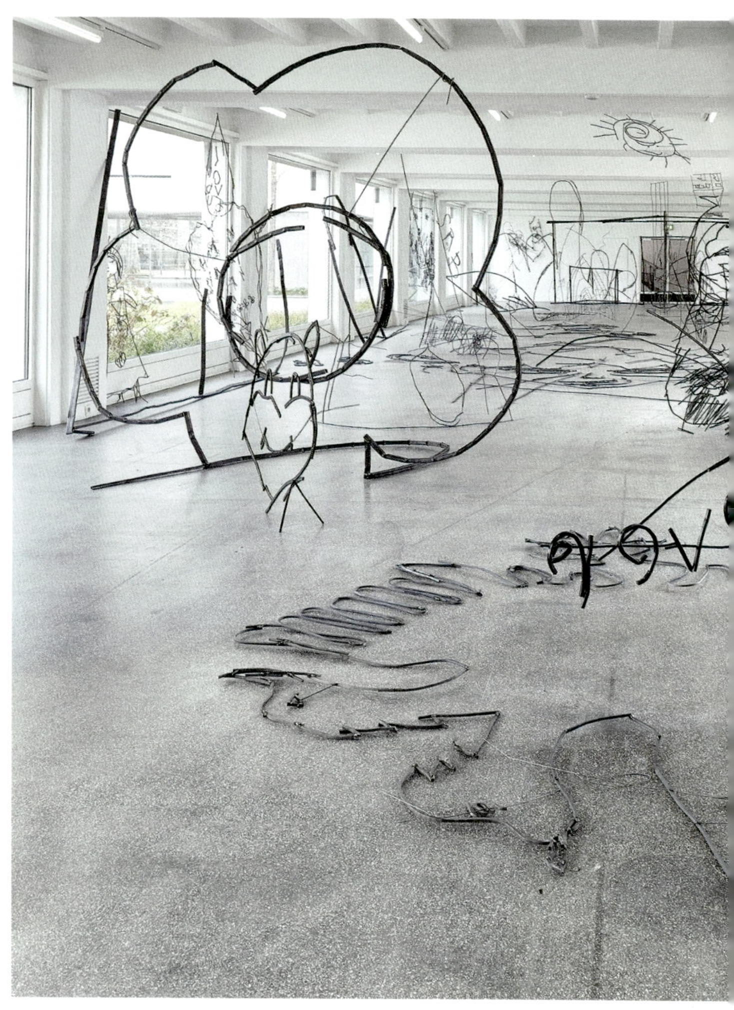

searched for language to describe—to diagnose—what this skipping might say about his orientation toward the world. Was it a disposition toward optimism? Did it suggest a desire for distraction, operating as a physical manifestation of a need for change, like scratching an itch? Or could it be that rare unconscious delight in pure presence, a predilection for play that the psychoanalyst D. W. Winnicott has described as self-healing, the primary site of creativity, and the condition for true discovery of the self?[1]

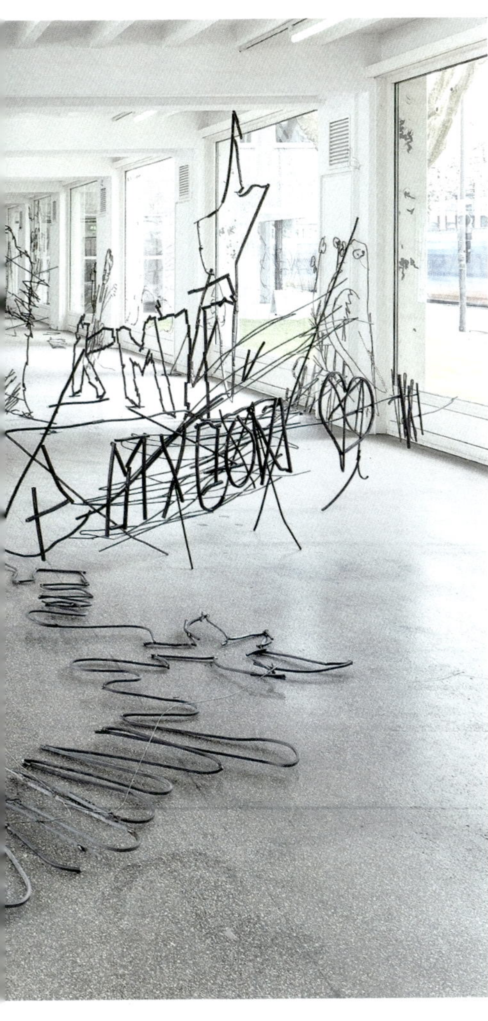

Fig. 4. **Petrit Halilaj**, *Abetare*, 2015. Installation view at Kölnischer Kunstverein, Cologne

Sharing conceptual DNA with his 2015 project at Kölnischer Kunstverein (fig. 4), Halilaj's Met project stems from his rediscovery of the desks at his former primary school, Shotë Galica in Runik. Intrigued by the graffiti and doodles that kids had scratched into the skin of the wood desks over the years, he began to make an archive of the anonymous etchings (fig. 5). His collection now includes images of planes, houses, cigarettes, phalluses, initials, hearts, comic book characters, rappers, bombs, and, of course, spiders. Halilaj renders

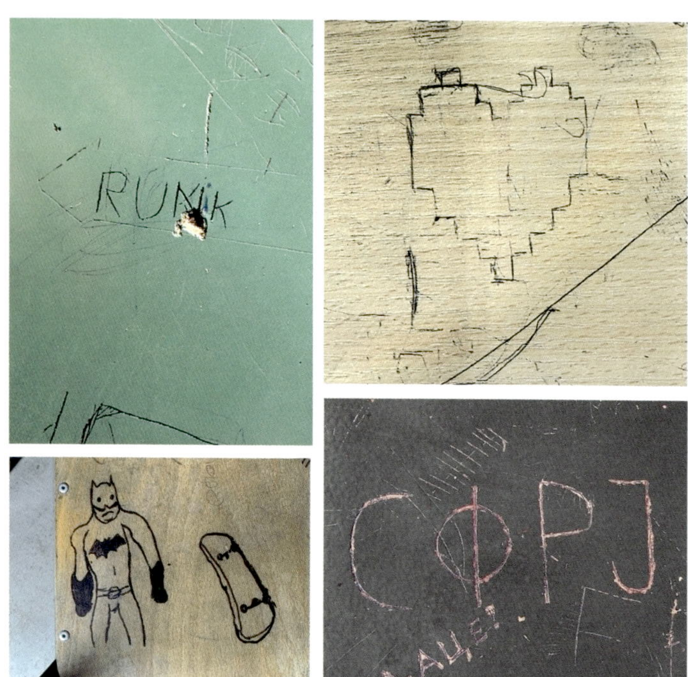

Fig. 5. Drawings and carvings from school desks in the Balkan region, catalogued during Petrit Halilaj's research for *Abetare*

these offhand drawings in bronze and steel, scaled up so that what were once near-immaterial shards of the imagination now create a reality that encompasses the viewer. There is an important elaboration of sources in his Met commission. Halilaj notes that while the original version focused exclusively on his hometown in Kosovo, the Met project entailed research to locate similar imagery at schools across the Balkan region, with his findings showing "the incredible diversity of the countries in the small area."[2] That diversity accounts for the various experiences of people living in a shared region plagued by war. For nearly a decade, from 1991 to 2001, the Balkans were brutalized by a series of conflicts stemming from the breakup of Yugoslavia and surging nationalist and ethnic tensions. Without flattening the complexity of these events, it can be said that a prevailing determinant in the course of the conflicts was the influence of Slobodan Milošević, whose government intended to replace the weakened Communist system with an ideology premised on Serbian nationalism. The UN reported that the Serbs, despite their contentions, aimed not to restore and reunify Yugoslavia,

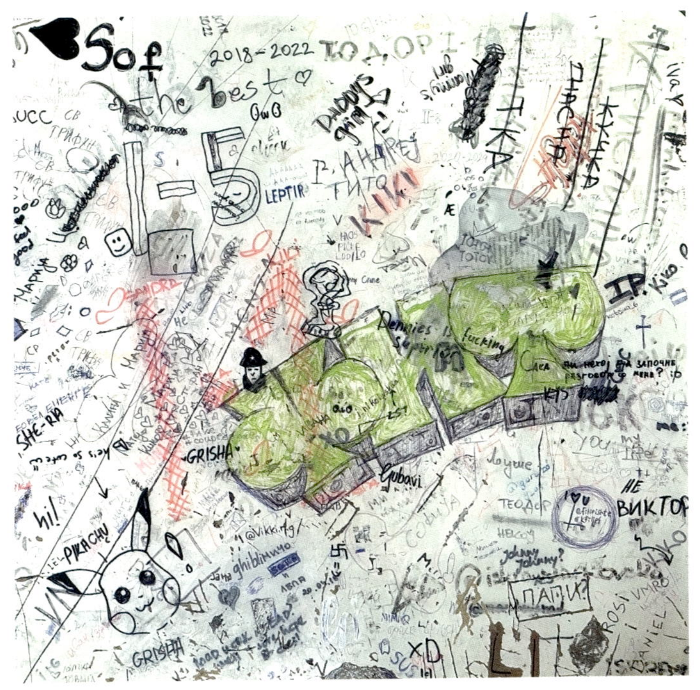

but rather to create a Greater Serbia.[3] Before the current campaign of aggression in Ukraine waged by the Russians, the wars in the Balkans were cited as Europe's deadliest conflict since World War II. In addition to nearly 140,000 casualties, this period was marked by Serbia's strategic persecution of ethnic minorities, including Kosovar Albanians like Halilaj. The UN established the International Criminal Tribunal for the former Yugoslavia (active 1993–2017) to prosecute "the gravest international crimes" since World War II, including genocide, ethnic cleansing, and mass rape and torture.[4] By opening his project up to experiences beyond his own geographic, national, and ethnic story, Halilaj complicates binary and purely oppositional categories that pit victor against loser, evil against good, nation against nation, or any one ideology against another, including "East" or "West"—none of which can ever fully accommodate the place and experience of the individual. As he notes, "For me, returning to the region and visiting numerous schools was prompted by a desire to construct my own intimate map, in contrast to historical maps that reflect dominant narratives. . . . We

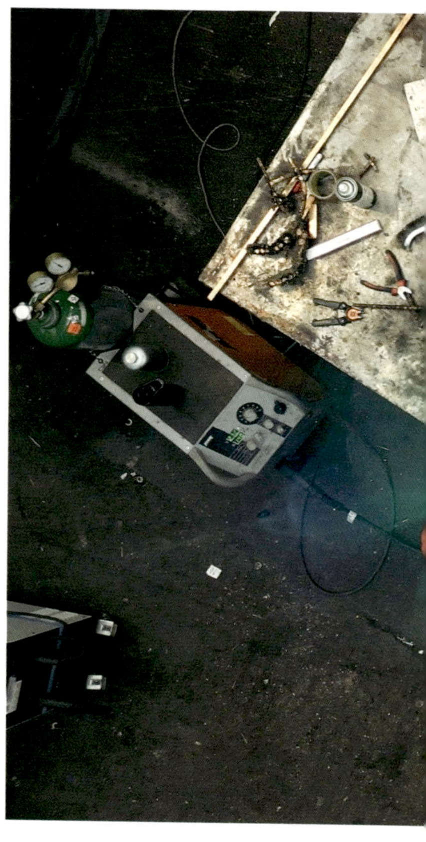

Fig. 6. **Petrit Halilaj** at work
on the fabrication of *Abetare*,
Berlin, 2023

do not exist in isolation. We are shaped by each other's identities, both positively and negatively."[5]

Considering the desperation of the history it navigates, Halilaj's project is a surprising and adamantly optimistic one. It is premised on the possibility of play—even, or especially, covert and illicit play—to imagine a future. This reordering of the world, privileging a child's place, has the potential to disorient. Prevailing sensibilities are challenged, and this begins with Halilaj's attention to a form of furtive mark-making whose very condition for existence is not being caught. The defiler of the desk makes their mark for a series of single, successive viewers, each person who sits in their place next. Not strictly private or public, neither purely anonymous nor clearly authored, this in-between status speaks to a kind of collectivity in which mak-

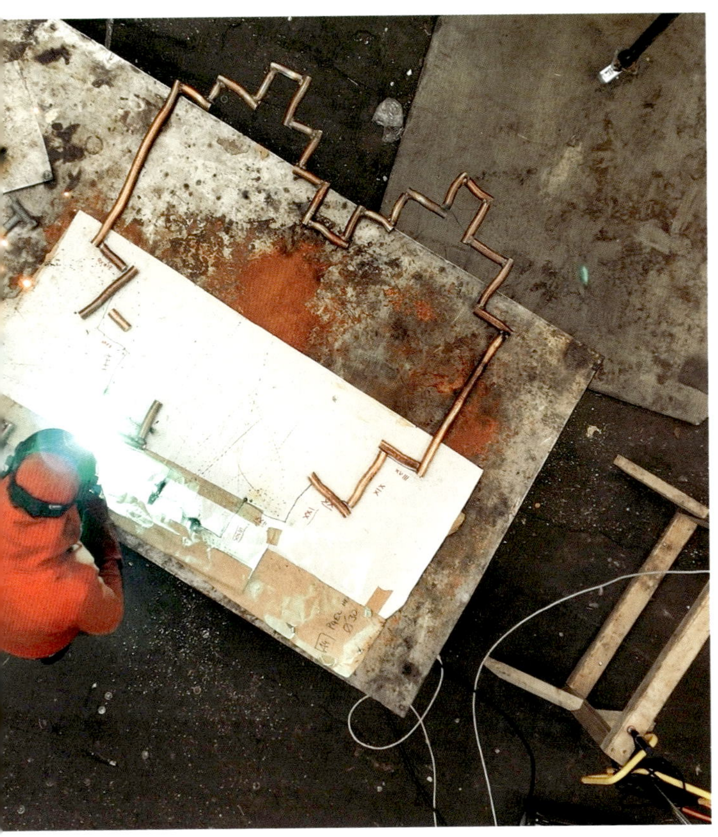

ing, seeing, and transforming are nearly indistinguishable. How many fantasies—drawings that live only in the mind—begin with the witnessing of image-yielding scratches like these? How many new scrawls are initiated as a response to what is already there, with subsequent individual contributions constituting a swerve, addition, or erasure and producing an artistic voice more choral than solo?

This tableau also makes a mess of chronology. Some historical markers—the name of a professional athlete or a celebrity—might help us periodize by height of popularity, but others are as timeless and ubiquitous as a crudely drawn penis. Time is leveled, made as flat as the desk itself. The impact of this corroded chronology is that the viewer cannot pathologize the collection of drawings. As much as a predilection for coherence might motivate a viewer to look for evidence of the

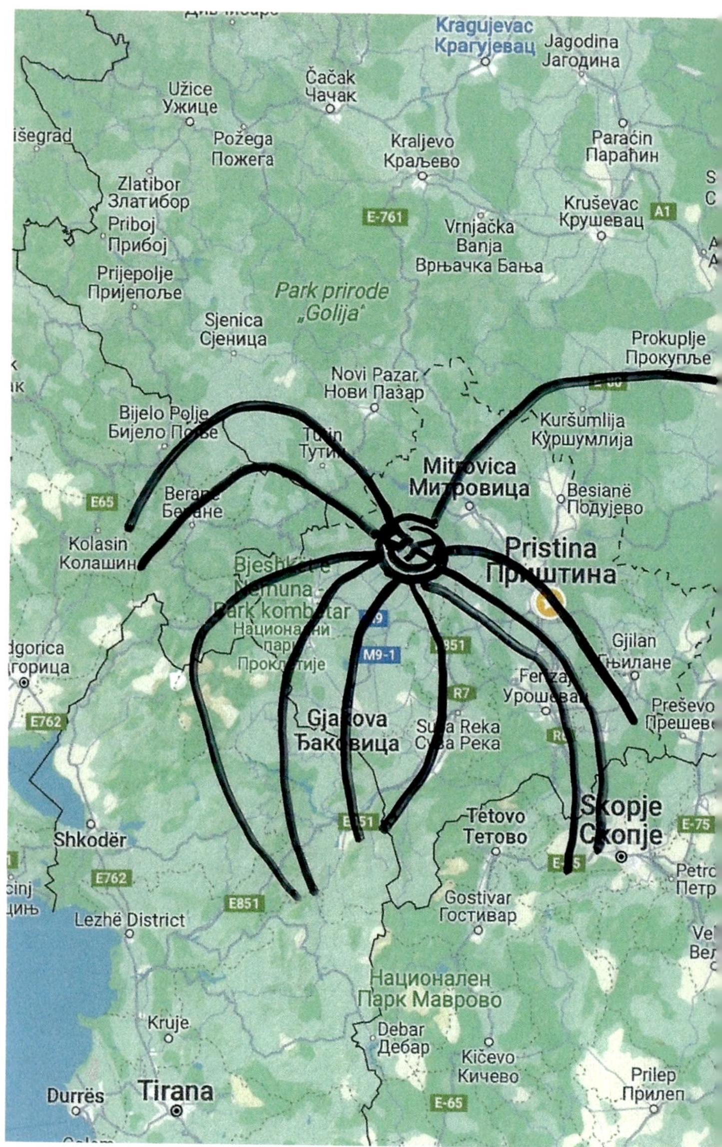

Fig. 7. **Petrit Halilaj**, map with artist interventions showing travel throughout the Balkan region during research for *Abetare*, 2023

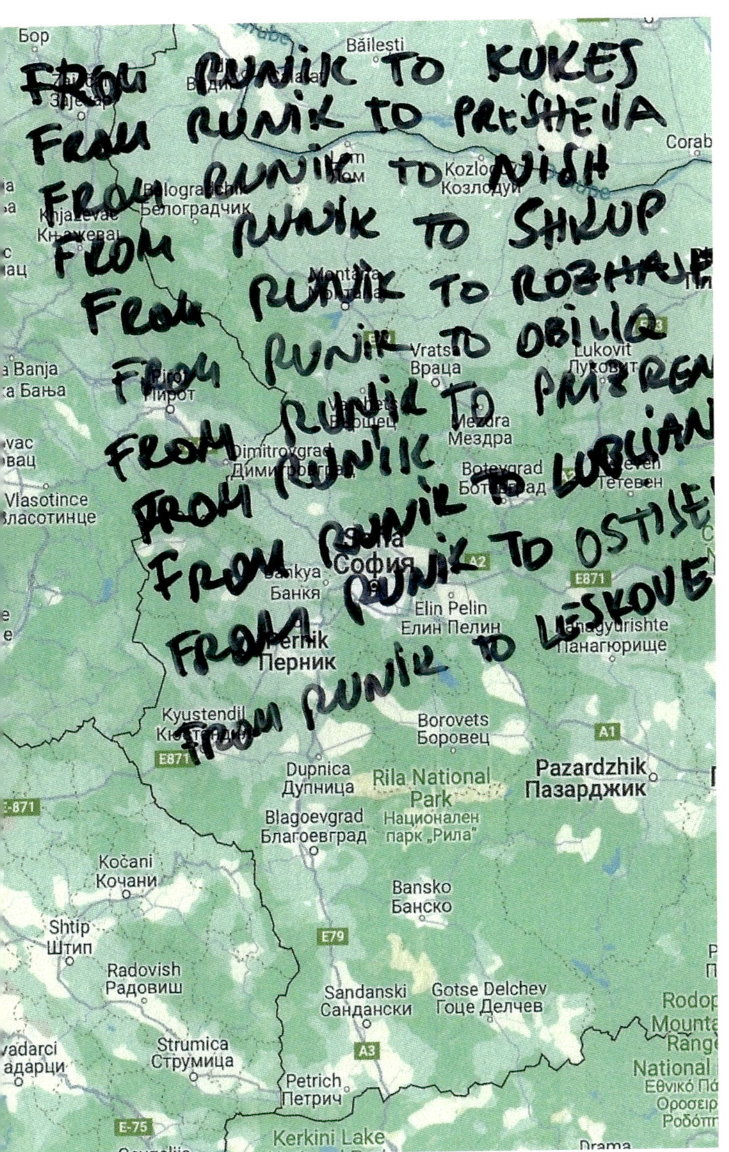
FROM RUNIK TO KUKES
FROM RUNIK TO PRESHEVA
FROM RUNIK TO NISH
FROM RUNIK TO SHKUP
FROM RUNIK TO ROZHAJE
FROM RUNIK TO OBILIQ
FROM RUNIK TO PRIZREN
FROM RUNIK TO LUBLJAN
FROM RUNIK TO OSTISE
FROM RUNIK TO LESKOVE

trauma that haunts "the Kosovar experience," this destabilizing of time, order, and sequence makes that reflex seem ridiculous—as if there is ever just a single, one-dimensional national or cultural experience. Any of these source drawings could have been created in a time of war, in a time of peace, in the before, after, or in-between. This destabilization also permits us to see childhood itself as multilayered and infinitely complex; here, tragedy, hope, fantasy, and reality all reside together in messy simultaneity.

When an international audience gathers in Manhattan to experience these works on The Met's roof, I am guessing that our first thoughts will not be about Halilaj's childhood. They might be about our own, or about the lives of children who are close to us. The cascade of connections is likely to bring us to those kids—in New York City, Kosovo, Venezuela, Ukraine, Palestine, Israel, from wherever we come, past, present, and future—whose childhoods are marked by impossible violence as well as unmitigated hope. We may consider the challenges of forging a self when the heat of the world conspires against the conditions that allow a self to set. But our looking might also kindle the memory of forgotten or repressed moments. The psychoanalyst Marion Milner wrote about the threshold between remembering and world making: "Moments when the original poet in each of us created the outside world for us, by finding the familiar in the unfamiliar, are perhaps forgotten by most people; or else they are guarded in some secret place of memory because they were too much like visitations of the gods to be mixed with everyday thinking."[6]

Back in Berlin, after we finished our lunch and studio visit, working on the model to stage some versions of what could be, Halilaj wanted to show me his neighborhood park. The playground buzzed with families, many of whom, he noted, were immigrants like himself. He delighted in the pandemonium of the scene, regaling me with facts about the money invested to create this expansive world dedicated to the pleasure of kids, the different designers who, freed from the fears of liability that neutered play for American children like me, built structures of such scale and precarity that they elicit those specific, perverse thrills that come only with the threat of injury. That glint of danger, Halilaj implied, made this place a form of utopia for him. A dangerous utopia? Is that utopia, I wondered? But why should one's reality, one's history, not contribute to what a perfect world could be? Why would utopia, or anything ardently wished for, not be forged from the fire of crisis? One of the most revelatory pieces of writing on the notion of child-as-artist and artist-as-child, and how art is shaped by life, can be found in Thomas Mann's novel *Doctor Faustus* (1947). The narrator relates the life story of his childhood friend, a modernist musician, speaking early in the book about what he has learned from observing him:

> The artist's life functions as the paradigm for how fate shapes all our lives, as the classic example of how we are deeply moved by what we call becoming, development, destiny. . . . The artist may remain nearer . . . childhood than the man who specializes in practical reality . . . nevertheless the artist's journey from those pristine early years to the late, unforeseen stages of his development is endlessly longer, wilder, stranger—and more disturbing for those who watch—than that of the everyday person, for whom the thought that he, too, was once a child is a cause for not half so many tears.[7]

After we finished our walk, we were deposited on the far side of the park. Halilaj waited for my ride to show and then, with a stutter of a skip, he disappeared back into the park and the playground. The future, if we are to have one, is already there.

Notes

1. D. W. Winnicott, *Playing and Reality*, 2nd ed. (London: Routledge, 2005), pp. 72–73.
2. See p. 36 in this volume for Iria Candela's conversation with Petrit Halilaj.
3. M. Cherif Bassiouni, "Final report of the United Nations Commission of Experts established pursuant to security council resolution 780 (1992), Annex IV – The policy of ethnic cleansing," United Nations, Dec. 28, 1994, https://web.archive.org /web/20120504142243/http://www.ess.uwe.ac.uk/comexpert/ANX/IV.htm.
4. United Nations, "International Criminal Tribunal for the former Yugoslavia," accessed January 22, 2024, https://www.icty.org/en/content/infographic-icty-facts-figures.
5. See p. 37 in this volume.
6. Marion Milner, as quoted in Winnicott, *Playing and Reality*, p. 52.
7. Thomas Mann, *Doctor Faustus*, trans. John E. Woods (New York: Vintage International, 1997), p. 28.

A Conversation with
Petrit Halilaj

Iria Candela

Iria Candela I thought we might begin by focusing on one of the smallest sculptures included in this installation: the arrow sign pointing to the north that reads "Runik." On several occasions you have dealt with issues of collective memory and cultural heritage related to your hometown, Runik, and more broadly to your homeland, Kosovo. You have worked with the former Natural History Museum of Kosovo and the Grand Hotel in Pristina; the early Neolithic settlements around Runik; the House of Culture in Runik; and now the school—your former school—in Runik. You have excavated the history of this village that was deeply affected by conflict and almost completely destroyed, including your family home, during the Kosovo War (1998–99), when Serbian forces expelled up to one million Albanians from Kosovo. However, in New York "Runik" is a foreign word lacking context. It is the name of a remote place, a small village that almost no one here knows or has heard of before—and yet it acquires great significance in this project when you decide to include it in this sign. What does the word "Runik" mean to you? What does it stand for here?

Petrit Halilaj For me, the word "Runik" holds a profound significance as a notion of home, for many reasons. However, given that I haven't lived there since 2004, it also evolves into a mechanism for questioning the very essence of "home." Runik transforms into a space for imagination, longing, and a void that I sense—a blend of distance and unfamiliarity that I experience simultaneously. I associate it with both notions of nesting and the act of flying away, encompassing all the contrast and friction inherent in this movement. In the sculpture, the word "Runik" is embedded in an arrow pointing in the direction of Kosovo. When I found this drawing on a child's school desk, I immediately felt that it would be a point of connection between where I found it and where it goes. So I think of it as a departure point.

IC You rarely begin a project from scratch in connection with an exhibition or a commission. You tend to do the reverse: bring a project along to the commission. Can you explain how you usually respond to a site or to an invitation to present your work?

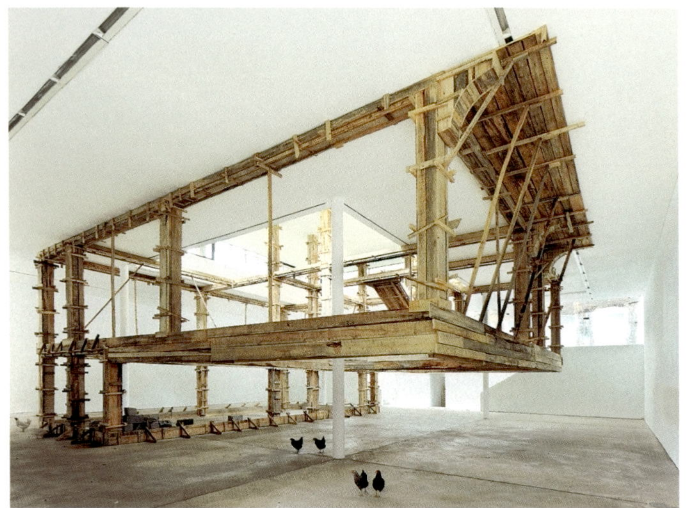

Fig. 8. **Petrit Halilaj**, *The places I'm looking for, my dear, are utopian places, they are boring and I don't know how to make them real*, 2010. Installation view at the 6th Berlin Biennale for Contemporary Art

PH The way I see it, exhibitions give us an opportunity to try to alter the course of personal and collective histories. They create complex worlds that claim space for freedom, desire, intimacy, and identity. Each new commission is a chance to explore, challenge, and imagine other possibilities—to question current configurations of reality and the way we make sense of our experience. I believe that things are interconnected in space and time, even when they seem fragmented at first sight. In creating a sculpture or a project, I build an open constellation of elements with the intention of allowing the audience the freedom to experience it from multiple angles, physically and mentally. I want people to have a chance to complete the fragmented realities that I stage—and that I am also trying to complete myself—even though they remain fundamentally impossible to grasp in their full complexity.

IC I have this recurring image of you always carrying your luggage, physically and metaphorically.

PH [He laughs.] Yes.

IC You're traveling with everything in your luggage. When we look at the chronology of your career, it becomes clear that although you have done many different things during a short period of time (which is quite extraordinary), the sequence is nonlinear. There is not a conventional development but rather a reoccurring in your projects. Some of your most complex works are realized multiple times in multiple sites—and this is one of those cases, *Abetare*—which adds a multidimensional sense of place and geography to your works.[1] They can be duplicated, repeated, and decontextualized, and somehow they are never resolute. They are never completely finished. What is particularly satisfying to you about this formula, of never reaching a resolution?

PH I think it has to do with giving space and trust to the audience and seeing this as an immense opportunity to talk about something, while also realizing its limits and acknowledging new questions that arise. If I think about the project at Tate St Ives, *Very volcanic over this green feather* (fig. 3), or *Abetare* itself, I realize that they evolve over time, and you can continue to pose new questions and understand them from different perspectives—in part because their origins are complex. In *Abetare*, for example, the sculptures are drawn from kids' doodles and engravings on school desks: they are acts of freedom (sometimes very intimate and anonymous

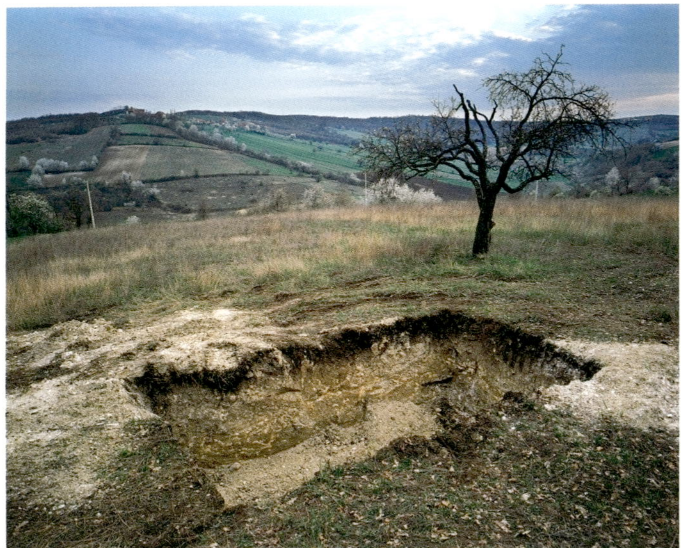

Fig. 9. **Petrit Halilaj**, *Kostërrc (CH)*, 2011. Sixty tons of Kosovo soil transported to Basel, Switzerland, for installation at Art Basel

acts), or ways to temporarily escape the educational system, which for a child usually represents not freedom but rather constraint through mandatory instruction. At the same time, school is a necessary phase to access an adult world. This is where we start learning who we are: how we write our names, how we relate to others, what our histories and identities are, and how we narrate and express those things. Schools begin structuring this complexity, while also flattening certain aspects of reality. The local educational system in Kosovo, for example, is strictly associated with the ideology of our national identity, with our affirmation of it. When I understood this, as an adult, I found it difficult to accept the simplifications of reality that come with ideology. As an artist, I see the exhibition as a space that allows me to rebuild the complexity. Similarly, the kids who make these drawings on the school desks are carving their own space of freedom. Yugoslavia went through a fall of the whole system. With it, the entire idea of education renovation fell apart. The desks are thirty, forty, even fifty years old—most of them are older than I am—and they contain layers of intergenerational expression. They have witnessed a massive change of ideology and system, and this transformation is preserved in the drawings. Sometimes you'll find a historical symbol that was written in the Communist era, an image that meant totally different things twenty years ago, and later kids have added lines that actually question it in a very funny way. It's fascinating to see these connections over time. When you look at these doodles and start to analyze them, you understand that they are not

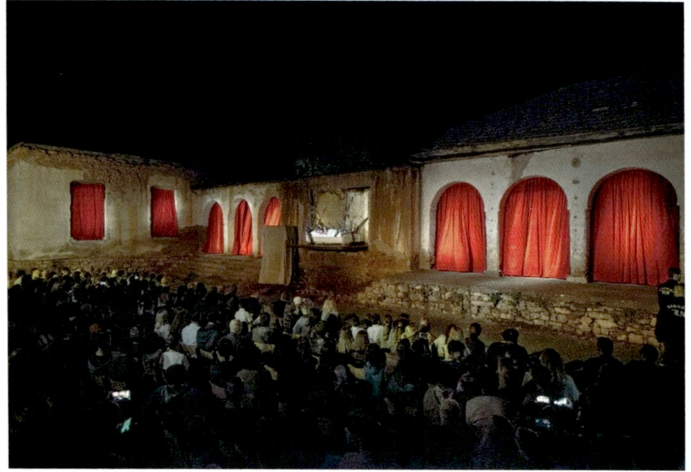

Fig. 10. **Petrit Halilaj**, *Shkrepëtima*, 2018. Installation view in Runik, Kosovo

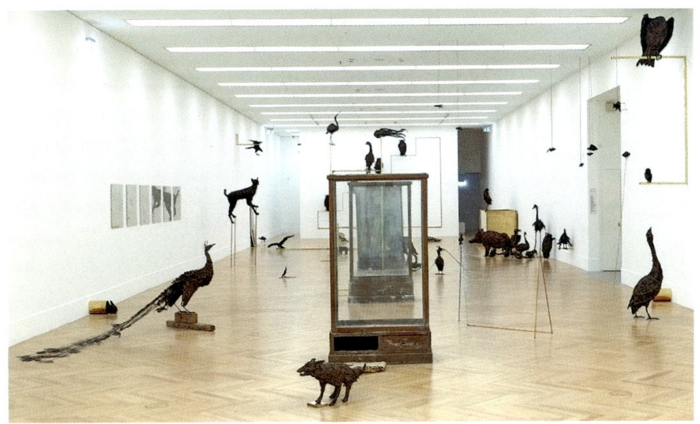

Fig. 11. **Petrit Halilaj**, *She, fully turning around, became terrestrial*, 2015. Installation view at the Kunst- und Ausstellungshalle der Bundesrepublik Deutschland, Bonn

linear. They carry a complexity of intervention and constant renovation, along with a certain level of destruction.

IC Let's go back to the beginning, to that moment of discovery, when you were visiting your former school in Runik. Can you tell us how you came across those desks in the first place?

PH Runik, where I grew up, is a very small town with few buildings that could be considered architectural landmarks: the elementary school, the high school, the former House of Culture, and the hospital. The rest are private houses. When I went back to visit my family one summer in 2010, I noticed that one of those landmarks, the school I attended as a child, was being destroyed. I could not grapple with the idea that we would demolish the few buildings that had endured the war rather than preserving them and the memories they carried. Other citizens, on the contrary, were happy about it. They said, "We'll have a new school building!" I went to the garden to film the final moments of the school, and a group of kids joined me (fig. 12). They showed interest in the camera, and I kept it on. In the resulting thirty minutes or so of video, you see these kids grabbing me and bringing me to the school for a last visit. One of them said, "Petrit, you should come and film this," pointing at the school desks that were piled up and ready to be thrown away. He said, "Everything is in them." I think the spark of the project was in this encounter between me—an adult pondering what we were losing with the destruction of this building—and the kids, who were just finding the best in that moment, accepting that they could not change it and having fun instead. They did what they would never normally be allowed to do at school: taking down images of the national hero Skanderbeg, going to the director's office, and painting all the walls and furniture everywhere.[2] They seemed to be enjoying a moment of revenge against not only the school but also the educational system as a whole, the constraints it symbolized and all the hard times it had given them. This is part of the spirit I wanted to preserve in the project.

IC   And it is titled *Abetare*. In earlier iterations and now here for the Roof Garden, you are bringing to life the collective memory of an anonymous group of children, past students who used those desks as platforms for self-expression. The desks' surfaces contain layers of inscriptions, scribblings, drawings, and doodles made over the course of many years, even decades. You choose to monumentalize them, to enlarge those drawings into three-dimensional sculptures and set them atop the museum, making them public. And with that gesture, you are calling attention to that transgressive, clandestine spirit you mentioned before, in the sense that the kids were breaking the rules, right? Writing on the desks is not allowed. You're destroying school property. [They laugh.] So it's not something that is particularly encouraged. Yet these are creative gestures by anonymous individuals who happen to be children and teenagers. Something interesting is taking place here, because your project is not only bringing to the fore the repressive, constrained routines of the school and the educational system but also addressing the art institution as represented by this museum: the art world and its own system of exclusions, no? In a sense there is something of an institutional critique unfolding here. It occurs to me that you're aligning your work with the work of those children, to somehow question the conventional assumptions concerning what constitutes a work of art. One of those conventions, for instance, is the accepted age at which an artist is considered an artist. As you know, museums don't usually include works made by children. Is this something that you think about? How much does the child in you still nurture the adult artist?

PH   You said it so beautifully that it's hard to add something. But I'll try. The title *Abetare* comes from the *ABC* book from which I learned the alphabet. The book is structured so that each letter of the alphabet has a lesson connected to it, with drawings and text. The letter *P* comes with the story of this boy, Petrit, who has chickens and a house: "Pulat e Petritit" (fig. 13). Back then, I thought that every

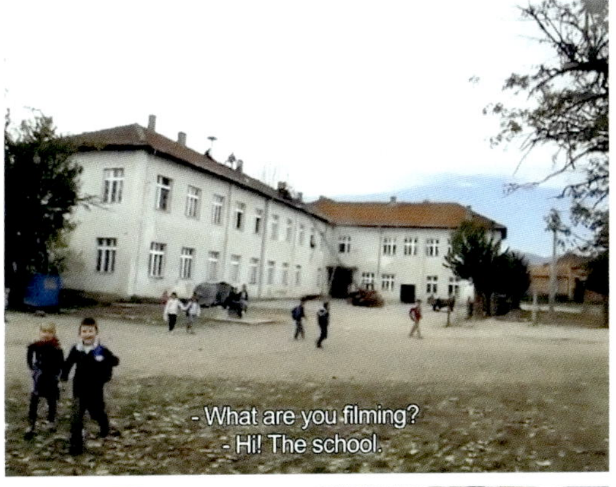

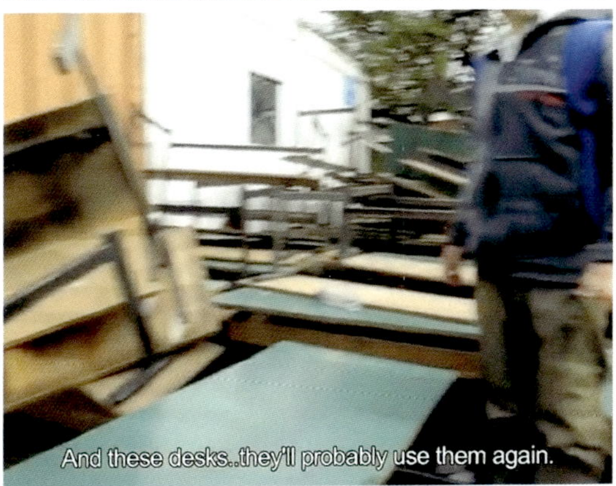

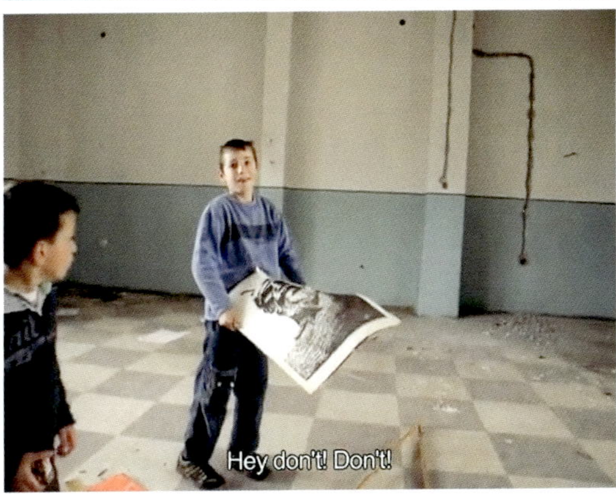

Fig. 12. **Petrit Halilaj**, video stills from *Abetare*, 2015. Digital video, 21 min., 53 sec.

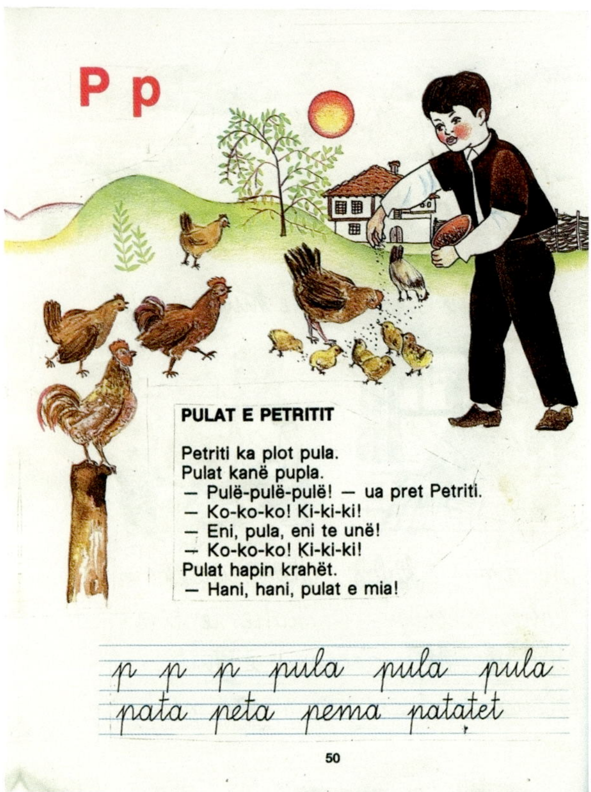

Fig. 13. Page corresponding to the letter *P* from *Abetare*, the alphabet book used by the artist at primary school in Kosovo

kid had a dedicated page in *Abetare*. My siblings' names were also there, so this seemed to confirm it. When I filmed the school, I became obsessed with finding a copy of *Abetare* (mine got lost when my house was burned down during the war) and the lesson with Petrit and the chickens. When I finally found it, I understood how dated it is. The drawings are an expression of Albanian socialist realism, so they represent a specific ideology—but also a precise historical moment, a geographical area, a language. How do you keep this tension between the book and the drawings, doodles, and scribbles on desks when you magnify them in scale? With the composition at The Met, I wanted to create an experience that evolves slowly in the encounter with unknown signs and symbols. Some of them might not be immediately understood in New York, because they are so historically rooted in their homeland. On the other hand, others are universal and immediately graspable. There are also references grounded in pop culture, sports, art, and cinema, and I hope these serve as a navigational tool to bring people into an experience of the exhibition.

IC   And this iconography, these universal symbols—they have always been there, and they are present in artworks at The Met, no? We can point to so many examples, from birds to crosses to hearts to flowers, such as the flowers of Andy Warhol (fig. 14). There are signs and symbols that have been present in the iconography of art history for centuries; people will recognize them from that context but also from their own school environments. You're developing a project that is so universal and at the same time so culturally and historically specific. This is something we've discussed: how you reconcile that "luggage" that you carry on your journeys—retain your unique identity and creative imagination, and the specificity of your homeland and its history—with a commission for a site that's an open roof terrace over-looking New York City, which is something of a global stage. That was one of the main challenges for you, right?

PH   Yes, absolutely. The sculptures that come together on the roof are also aimed at questioning the centrality of certain historical narratives, bringing together a complex symphony of frag-ments. They disrupt notions of scale and occupy unexpected spaces, existing in opposition to the idea of a central, monumental piece. They follow my desire to trust that things are interconnected. I should

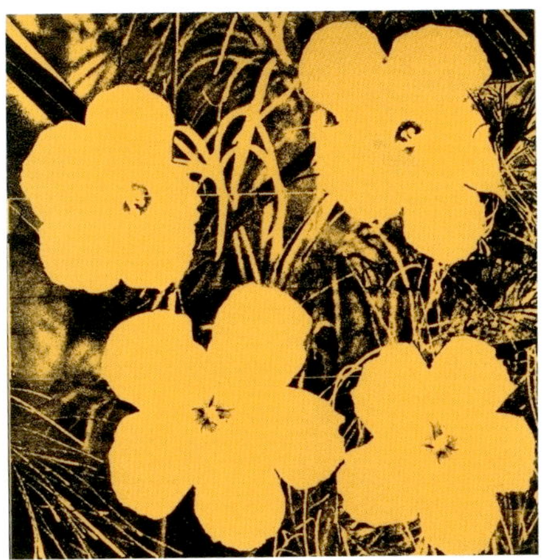

Fig. 14. **Andy Warhol**, *Flowers*, 1967–68. Acrylic and silkscreen enamel on canvas, 9 ft. 7 1/4 in. × 9 ft. 7 1/2 in. (292.7 × 293.4 cm). The Metropolitan Museum of Art, New York, Gift of Mr. and Mrs. Peter M. Brant, 1979 (1979.549)

clarify that the original version of *Abetare* was exclusively focused on Kosovo—Runik—while the Met commission stems from extended research across the Balkan region, including Albania, Bosnia and Herzegovina, Croatia, Kosovo, Montenegro, North Macedonia, Serbia, and Slovenia. The drawings I found come from very different geographies and languages. They show the incredible diversity of the countries in the small area of the Balkans. There are different religions, local "heroes," and historical symbols, but also a lot of common ones, some of which seem to be universal. There's [Lionel] Messi, Pac-Man, and transnational references to pop culture and cinema. And then there's a layer I add: for example, when I found the doodle of a spider in Skopje (fig. 15), I immediately thought of the art of Louise Bourgeois. I saw this element coming alive as a creature. It's been fascinating to notice what a different sense of "home" I've developed in recent years, through the artists I admire, the spaces that shaped me, the artworks that made me who I am today. This new sense of belonging makes me feel at home not only in Runik but in many places. So I thought, how did my connection to Runik change? How can I reconnect this with the luggage of past experience? I was born in Kosovo, became a refugee in Albania. I can remember going on holiday to Montenegro with my family, before the war. All these references and fragmented memories are present, but then I find a spider doodle on a school desk, and I think of Louise Bourgeois. So I feel home differently—connecting to the world through contemporary art. That, for me, was magical.

IC   You started to have new family members, this time by choice. It's interesting, the idea of starting to find yourself home elsewhere and finding a home in museums. I feel that way, too. Whenever I'm in a museum, I feel at home somehow. You spoke about *Abetare* expanding into other areas of the Balkans. As you say, the drawings are universal expressions of desires, love, fantasies, fears, and trauma. At the same time, you have chosen to include, for example, the abbreviation KFOR, which, for a local person, would immediately bring back memories of war, of the Kosovo Force's efforts to secure the space for Albanians to return home.[3] The drawings that you source from the school desks are all anonymous. We don't know anything about the people who made them. Who are they? Where are they now? You're also appropriating them to make your own story, as you explained. The story has recently been broadened because, for the first time, for this particular project at The Met, you decided to expand your research to schools in other countries that were once part of the former Yugoslavia. What did you bring back from these trips? In what ways has that research expanded the project?

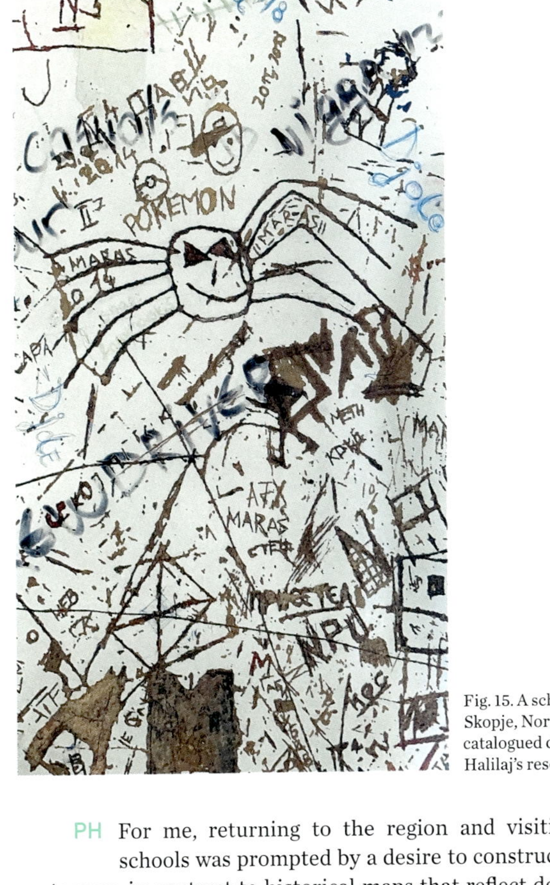

Fig. 15. A school desk in Skopje, North Macedonia, catalogued during Petrit Halilaj's research for *Abetare*

PH For me, returning to the region and visiting numerous schools was prompted by a desire to construct my own intimate map, in contrast to historical maps that reflect dominant narratives. The endeavor challenges established borders and geographies that impose limits on our freedom of movement. Much like spiders create their webs for survival, my map serves as a means of making sense by connecting the dots. I came to realize that it's not sufficient to be concerned only with one's own identity. We do not exist in isolation. We are shaped by each other's identities, both positively and negatively. In Kosovo, for example, I have sought to reexamine identities, maps, and geographies by infusing them with new perspectives, sometimes in a personal manner—sharing fresh narratives about what we already know in an area whose history has been marked by numerous conflicts, including the ideological clash between East and West.

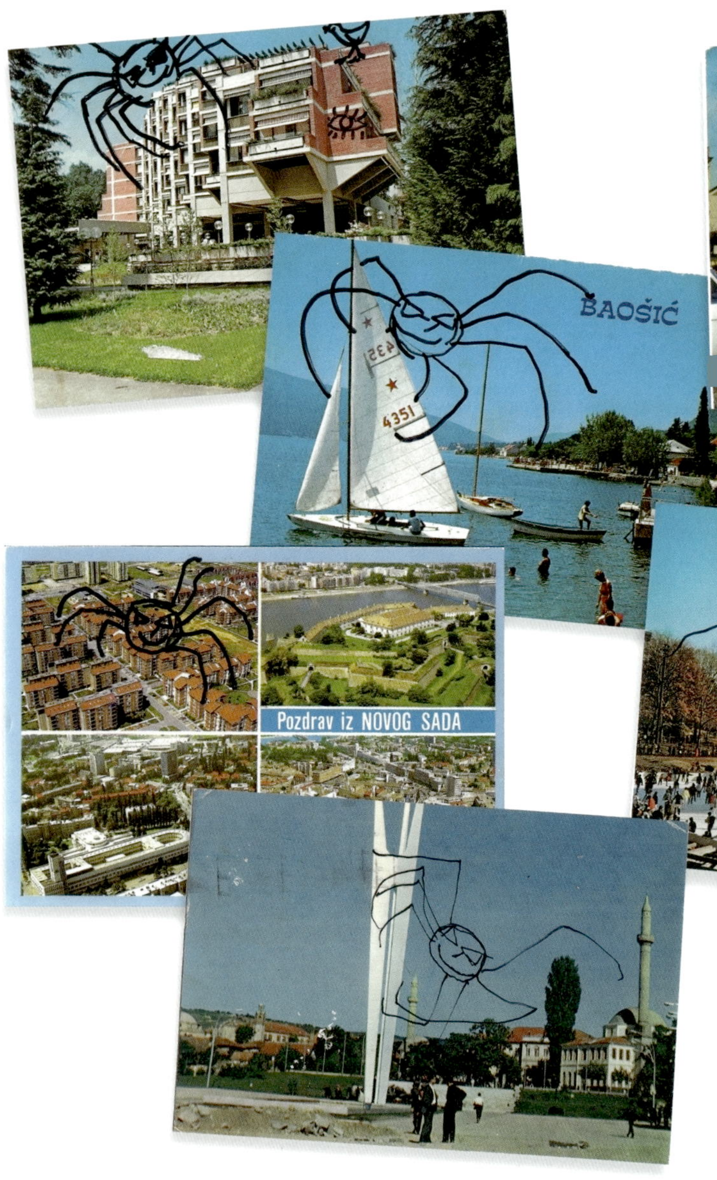

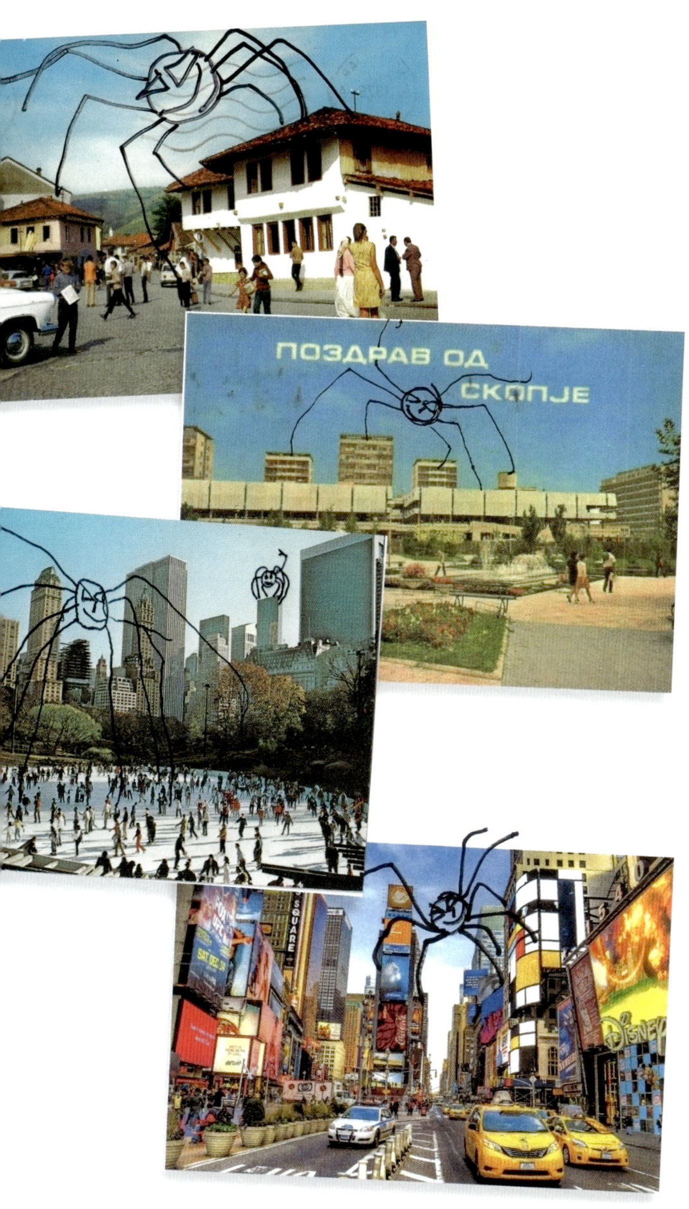

ПОЗДРАВ ОД
СКОПЈЕ

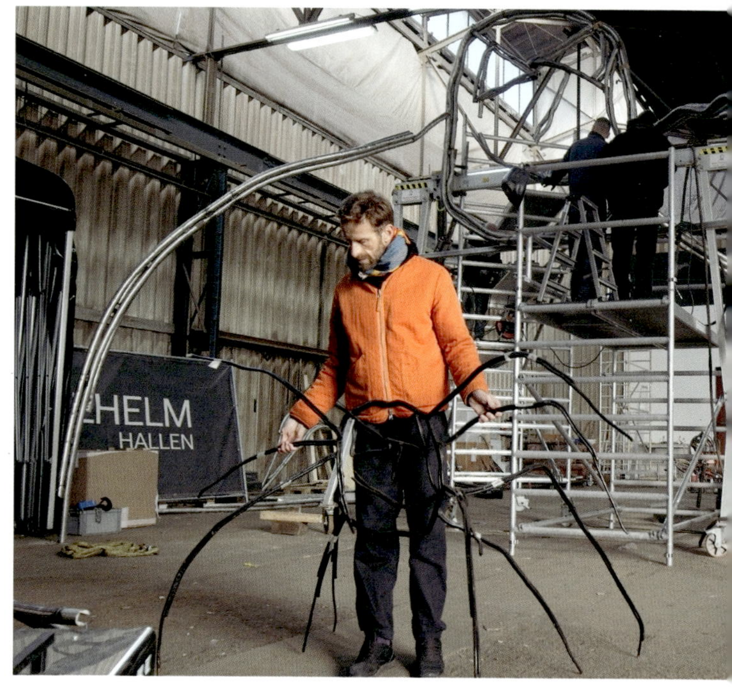

Initially, when composing a list of places to visit, I considered going to Serbia, but personal limits rooted in my wartime experiences held me back. When I thought of encountering the Serbian police or forces at the border with Kosovo, I realized I wasn't ready yet. Nevertheless, my commitment to including Serbia led to research conducted by someone else, specifically in local schools at Novi Sad, Preševo, and Tërnavë. Despite my inability to visit personally, I appreciate that works based on those drawings will coexist with others here, supporting each other. In a way, the installation challenges my personal boundaries, bringing together elements I'm not yet ready to reconcile on a personal level.

IC We discussed earlier how working outdoors has prompted a change of scale. You've decided to embrace shifts in scale with this work. In particular, you have chosen to enlarge the house and the spider above the rest of the drawings. Yet there's not an intended hierarchy in the iconology, in the reading of these images, just because of their size or position in the installation. There is a democratic sense

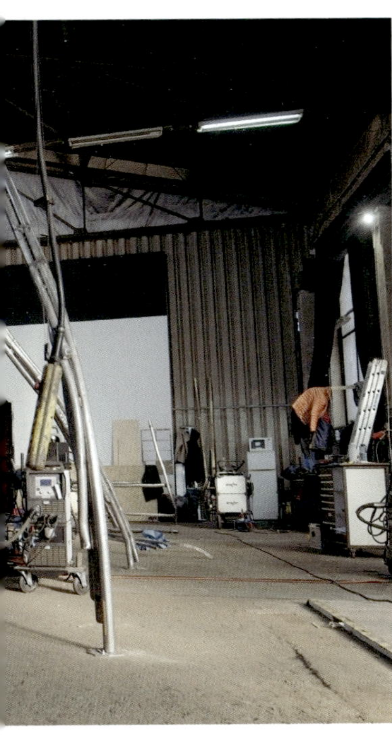

Fig. 17. **Petrit Halilaj** at work
on the fabrication of *Abetare*,
Berlin, 2023

that they all participate in the orchestra, and that they each have their own significance and make their contribution to the whole narrative. Let's talk then about how you place things, because the way your work occupies the Roof Garden is new with regard to previous commissions there. Your sculptural program is decentered, occupying the whole space to the edges, even overflowing the container of the terrace. This is consistent with a long-standing preference of yours to create a sort of stage, an environment that comes out of your imagination but gets concretized in the physical space to allow others to participate in it. Can you describe your creative process, or the method by which your initial mental images come into realization?

PH When I received the invitation for this commission, I was intrigued by the idea of bringing an expanded version of *Abetare* here. I aimed for the sculptures to transform into standing drawings within the space, sparking a novel relationship and dialogue with the environment, the landscape, and the city. For instance, take the spider sculpture: I envision it as reminiscent of war-themed

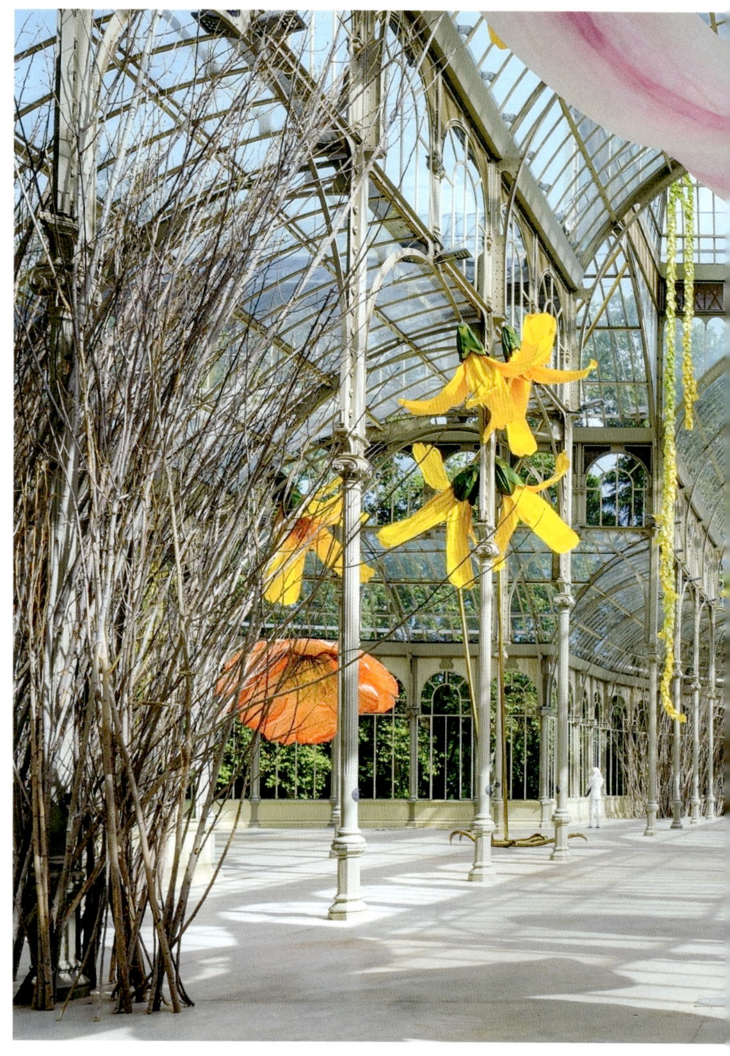

Fig. 18. **Petrit Halilaj**, *To a raven and hurricanes that from unknown places bring back smells of humans in love*, 2020. Installation view at Palacio de Cristal, Museo Nacional Centro de Arte Reina Sofía, Madrid

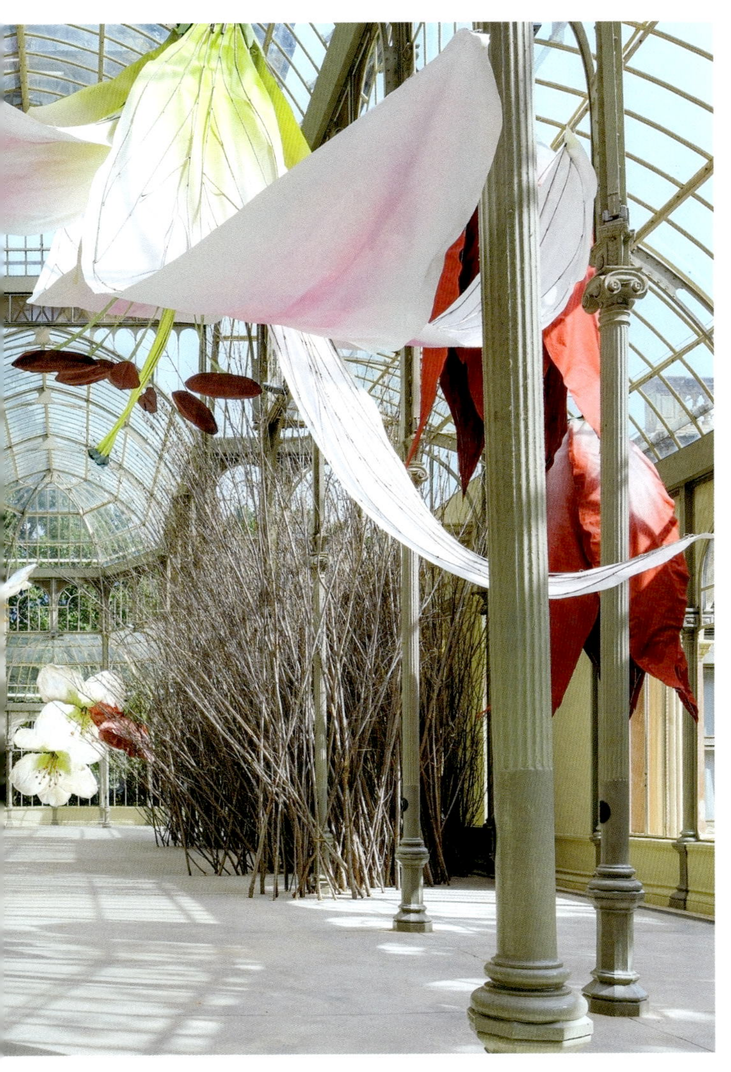

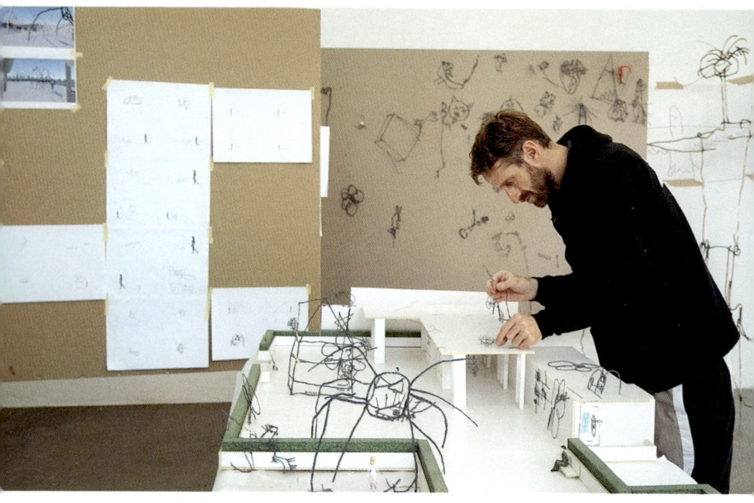

Figs. 19–20. **Petrit Halilaj** at work on a model of *Abetare*, Berlin, 2023

storylines in which alien or mutated tentacular creatures threaten the city, traversing its heights—like in the film *War of the Worlds* [2005]. I believe there's a moment when the size of certain sculptures aligns perfectly with their personality in a given space and brings them to life in connection with the surroundings. For me, the spider finds completeness in its interaction with the city, altering our perception of it. This is why some of the drawings are enlarged—to enhance this dynamic connection. Reflecting on Yugoslavia's centralized system, with a distinct center and ideology, I wanted to highlight that Kosovo was far from the center of that ideological narrative; we were the marginalized, the unheard voices. So here I deliberately avoided creating a monumental centerpiece for viewers to focus on. Instead, I aimed for people to recognize the significance of what we term the "periphery"— the concurrent stories and voices that speak alongside the dominant narratives. Additionally, the house is sculpturally crafted as a three-dimensional collage that incorporates numerous drawing fragments from diverse areas—the cloud, the shooting star—all sustaining each other. Without each of these elements, the house would fall. This approach, unprecedented in the *Abetare* project, required me to take responsibility for combining drawings in such a way that they provide physical support to each other as structures in space, so that the whole is capable of enduring extreme weather conditions like hurricanes. (For security reasons, in fact, the sculpture had to be able to endure a

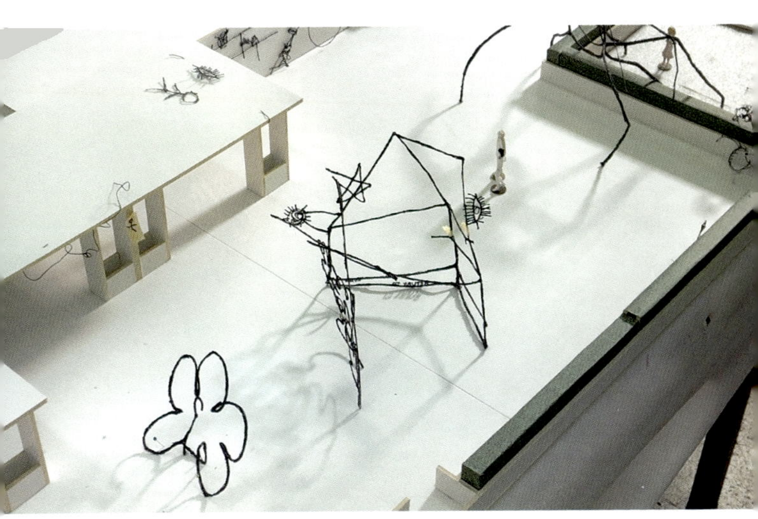

hurricane, by contract! All our calculations were made based on that.) Metaphorically, the resilience of the combined fragments embodies the idea that only by bending and mutually sustaining each other can we navigate extreme conditions together.

IC   And yet they are vulnerable in their transparency, in the way they are scattered around, blending with the surrounding space.

PH   As you rightly mention, the sculptures possess transparency, a distinct presence, but also a void. They sketch out a space without confines, allowing us to construct and envision space within and through them. This approach is true to the original contexts in which the drawings were found. Placing the sculptures in unexpected spaces—behind walls, in areas not conventionally designed for exhibitions—is a deliberate choice. In doing this, we challenged the existing structures that had defined previous commissions. It's an unconventional approach that became integral to the essence of this specific project.

IC   That's very important, as is what you've said about the decentralizing—kind of contesting the monument and all its implications. So let's talk about the *faktura*, the making and the

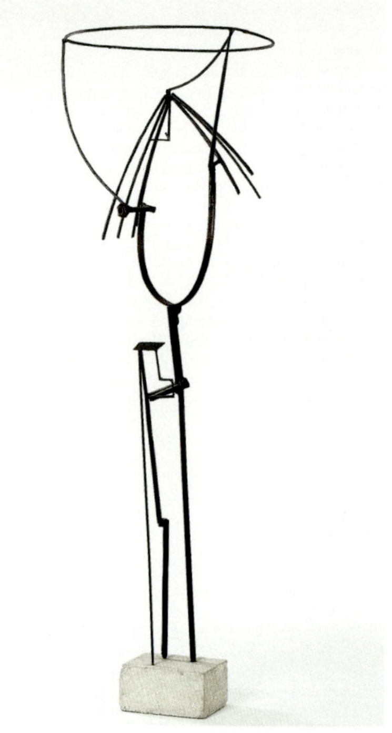

Fig. 21. **Julio González**, *Woman with the basket* (*Femme a la corbeille*), 1934. Wrought iron, stone base, H. 67 ¾ in. (172 cm). Musée National d'Art Moderne, Centre Georges Pompidou, Paris

medium you use, which has its genealogy in the sculptures, or "drawings in space," that the Spanish artist Julio González made in the 1920s and 1930s by bending and welding metal (fig. 21). Their lack of gravitas and absence of volume revolutionized the sculptural field. Artists like [Alexander] Calder, Gego [Gertrud Goldschmidt], and Ruth Asawa would follow that track. This idea seems to align with your aim to achieve a sense of lightness, even in three-dimensional sculptures made by welding stainless steel and bronze. Perhaps this is a way to counter the pathos linked to a difficult, traumatic past (that luggage!)— the sense of weightlessness that you've employed before in your floating houses, flying creatures, hovering structures, hanging images. Is this a conscious decision?

PH Yes, I see this search for lightness as a means to counterbalance the heaviness inherent in certain contexts. The original rendition of *Abetare* was crafted from steel, a material available for architectural construction (used in reinforced concrete) that can be purchased in lines and subsequently bent into a structure that invisibly supports an entire finished building. Steel is not traditionally considered a noble material, but it retains a certain essence reminiscent of the simplicity found in the desk drawings—the gesture, the longing to leave a mark somewhere. When it came to creating the outdoor version of *Abetare* for The Met, a shift to a different material was essential, and I opted for bronze in addition to stainless steel. It was somewhat surprising to discover that even bronze, a material with a more esteemed status in art history, is also produced in lines, and thus the sculptures did not have to be cast to be realized. It was a very sculptural process: challenging the lines until they broke, bending them until they sustained the curve. Metaphorically, this aspect became quite intriguing to me—exploring the extent to which a straight line could be challenged and bent before reaching its breaking point.

IC   As you're describing this, I'm reminded that this is kind of the first time you're doing work outdoors. Well, there is your summer 2022 project for Manifesta (fig. 22), which involved a transformation of the sign atop the Grand Hotel in Pristina, a former five-star hotel whose declining condition over the years mirrored the fall of Yugoslavia. But this is your first outdoor project of this scope—the first iteration of *Abetare* realized completely outdoors. We spoke about the challenges that you faced here. Do you think this will mark a new path in your career? You were saying how many things you have learned about the logistics, but do you also think this is something that will take you further in engaging with outdoor space and public space?

PH   Yes, definitely. The first time I presented *Abetare*, at the Kölnischer Kunstverein, only one sculpture (the rocket) was outdoors—in the museum's courtyard. I've come to more fully understand how different and challenging it is to work outdoors. Until now I struggled to find a convincing way to bring the project outside; I believed its strength lay in challenging indoor perspectives and disrupting our sense of orientation by overlaying the lines of the drawings onto the architecture of a room. Bringing *Abetare* to The Met's roof meant relating to the building's architecture and the New York skyline. This was very new to me, and it required a long period of questioning. The primary challenge was how to infuse the outdoor *Abetare* with the same layering and complexity achieved in the indoor context. The outdoor piece you mentioned, *When the sun goes away, we paint the sky*, was built the other way around: you had to experience the city from different angles to be able to read the whole sentence, and it was never fully legible from any one single point of view. It relied on the

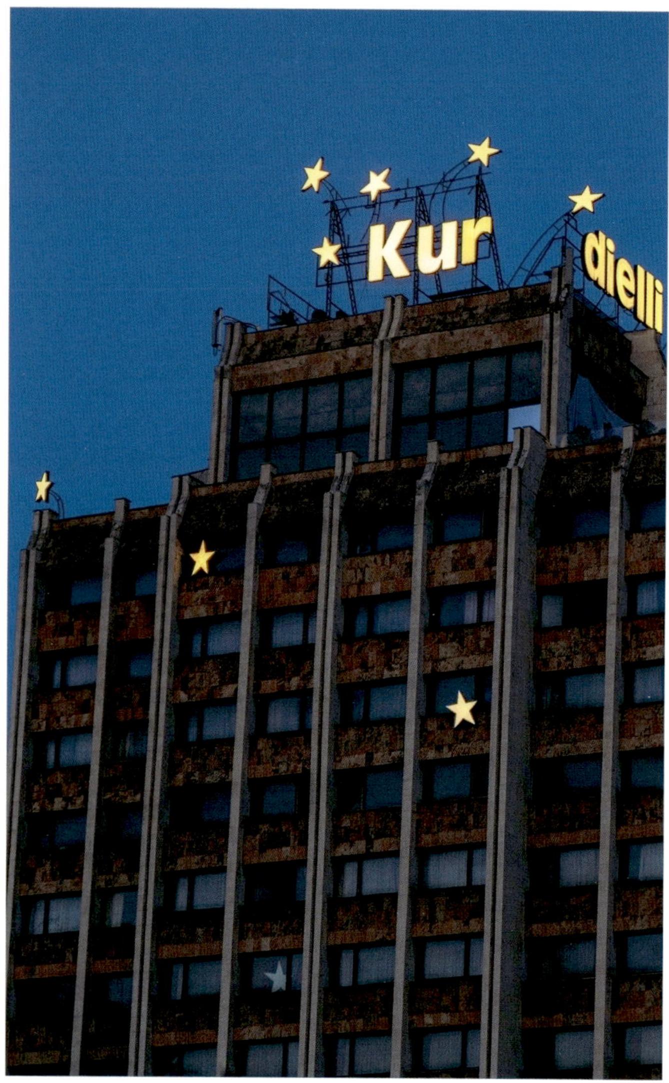

Fig. 22. **Petrit Halilaj**, *When the sun goes away, we paint the sky (Kur dielli të ikë do ta pikturoj qiellin)*, 2022. Installation view at Manifesta 14, Pristina, Kosovo

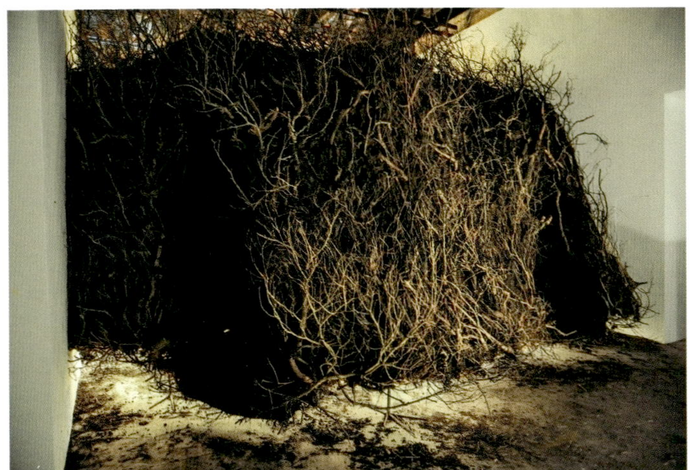

Fig. 23. **Petrit Halilaj**, *I'm hungry to keep you close. I want to find the words to resist but in the end there is a locked sphere. The funny thing is that you're not here, nothing is*, 2013. Installation view at the Kosovo Pavilion at the 55th Venice Biennale

viewer's memory; people had to retain a fragment they saw from the west side of the city ("we paint the sky") until they encountered the other piece, from a different street ("when the sun goes away").

IC   This is a nice segue to my last question. Your recent projects have dealt less with the past and your biography, and more with experiences rooted in the present or looking to the future. We spoke about the parallels between your personal identity and the cultural identity of the young country of Kosovo. You're participating in a fight for LGTBQ rights there and the founding of a new museum of contemporary art in Pristina. During a recent conversation, you said there's still opportunity in Kosovo to set the path for the future, especially in terms of achieving equal rights and freedoms. Can you elaborate on this emerging role as an activist?

PH   I would not dare to define myself as an activist, although my work could be labeled "soft activism." I have great respect for the work real activists do, their uncompromising commitment to civil society. But with my work I try to support it as much as I can—for example, in the approval of a new civil code in Kosovo, allowing equal rights to all citizens, regardless of gender identity and sexual orientation. Our collaborative journey, Iria, in realizing this commission together, was incredibly enriching for me. I found it fascinating that

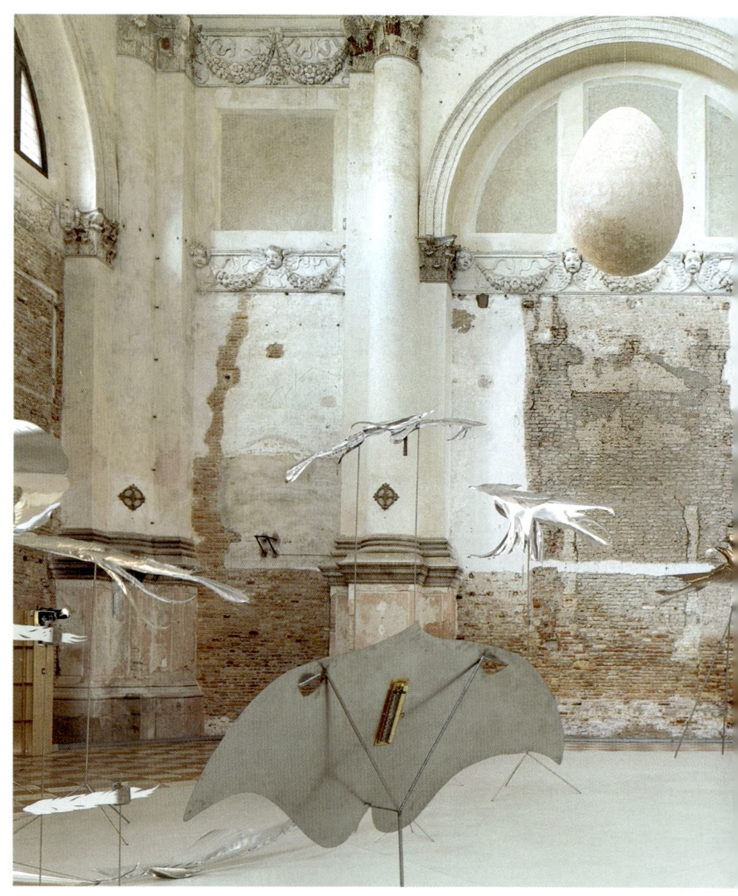

you hadn't been to Kosovo and hail from a different context that lacks a direct connection—much like the majority of individuals who will visit the roof. It's a geographically specific area with a tumultuous recent history, a young country undergoing significant transformations. For me, the unknowns and the opportunities to carve out a space and advocate for freedoms, reflected in the very process of this commission, are both beautiful and challenging, and undeniably exhilarating. I'm grateful to be a part of this experience. Years ago, I was trying to escape from "home," in a way, evading the weight of memories that felt like a hindrance to self-discovery. Now, with more experience (and years), I can face it and even embrace it once more, and I'm genuinely happy to do so. I feel ready!

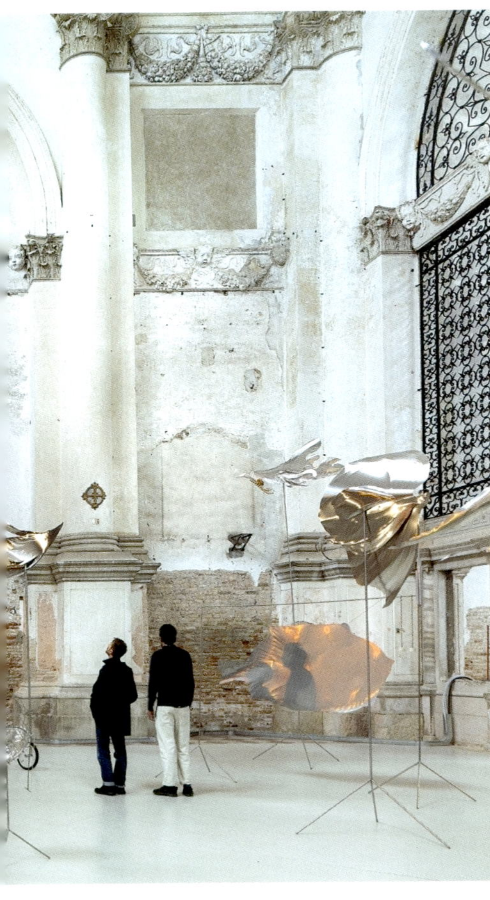

Fig. 24. **Petrit Halilaj** and **Álvaro Urbano**, *Lunar Ensemble for Uprising Seas*, in *Thus waves come in pairs*, 2023. Installation view at TBA21–Academy's Ocean Space, Venice

Notes

1. A first iteration of *Abetare* was presented at the Kölnischer Kunstverein, Cologne, April 14–August 2, 2015.
2. Skanderbeg (Gjergj Kastrioti, 1405–1468) was an Albanian military commander celebrated for coordinating a successful resistance of Ottoman Empire forces.
3. The Kosovo Force (KFOR) is a NATO-led military force deployed in Kosovo since 1999 to ensure peace and stability in the region.

Abetare, 2024

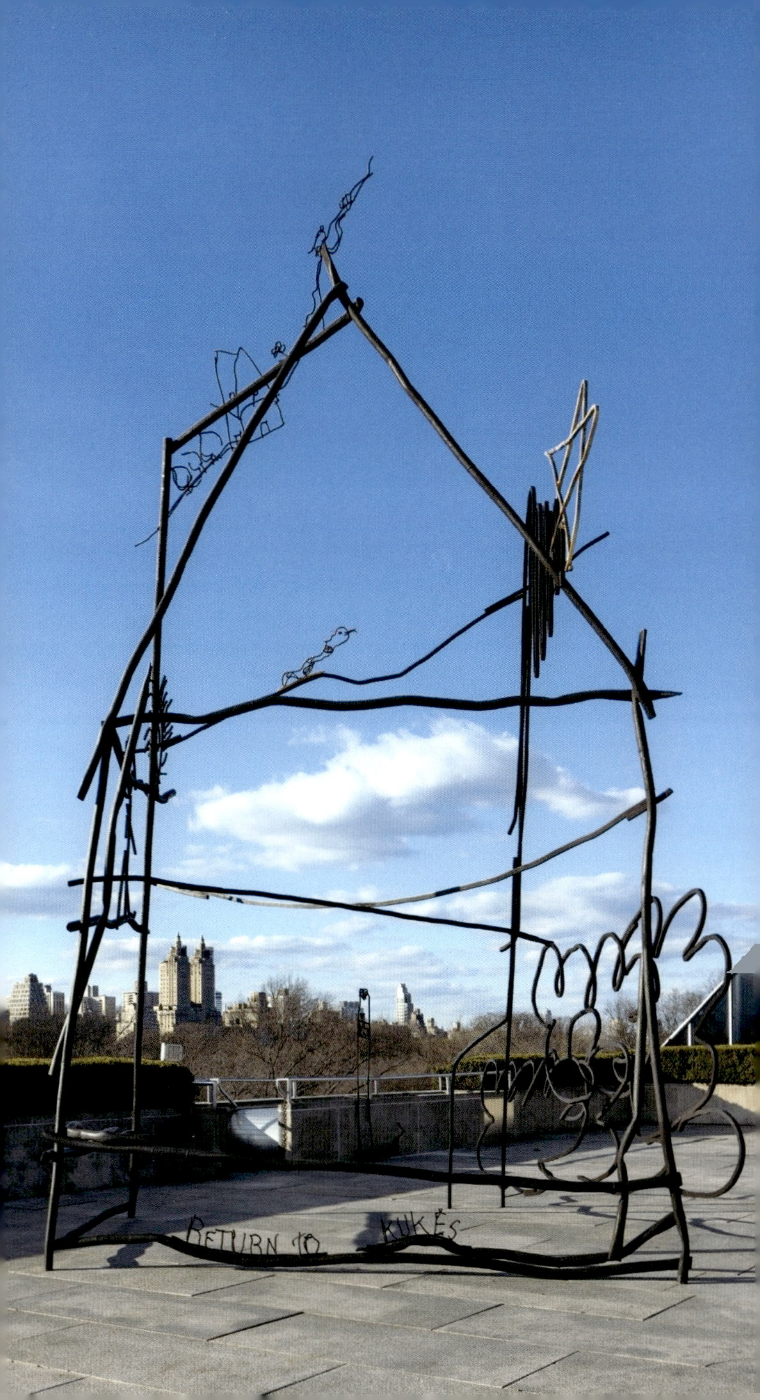
RETURN TO KUKËS

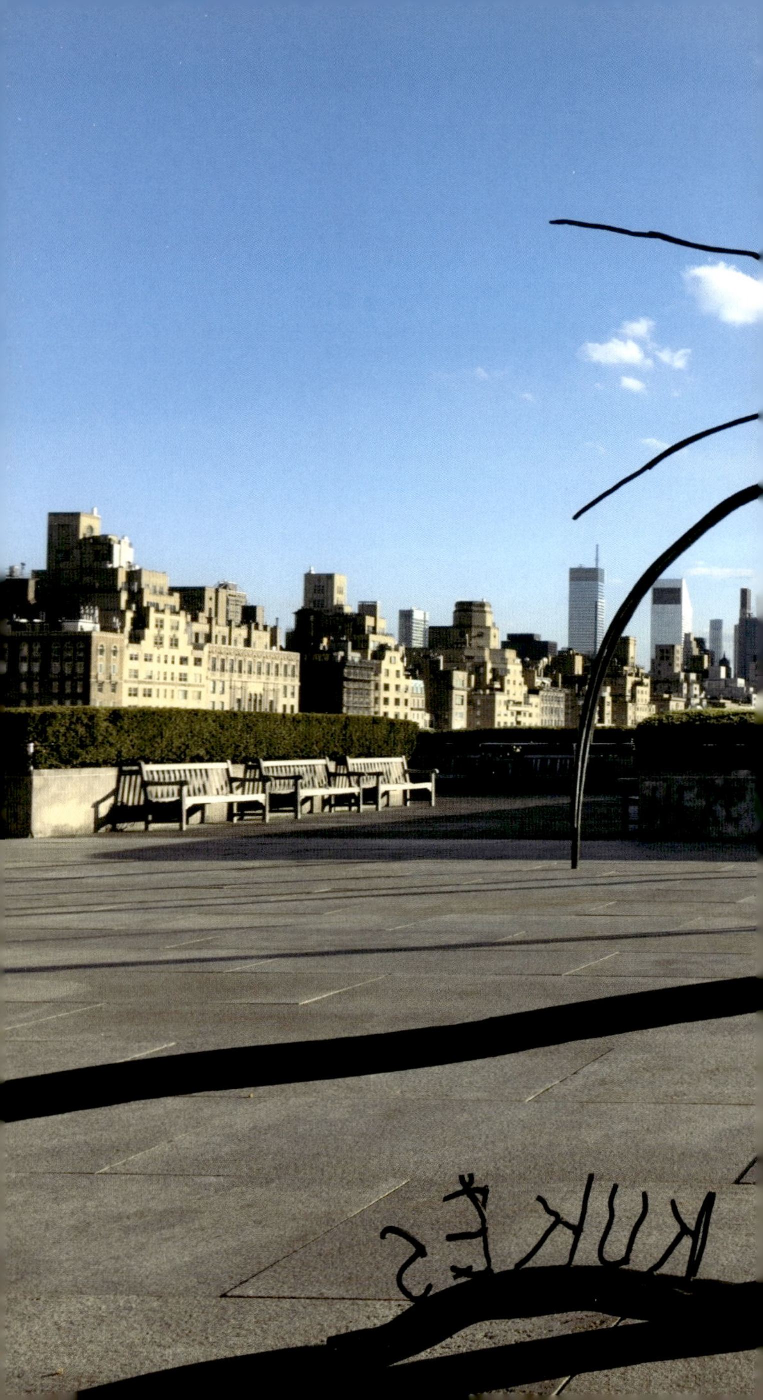

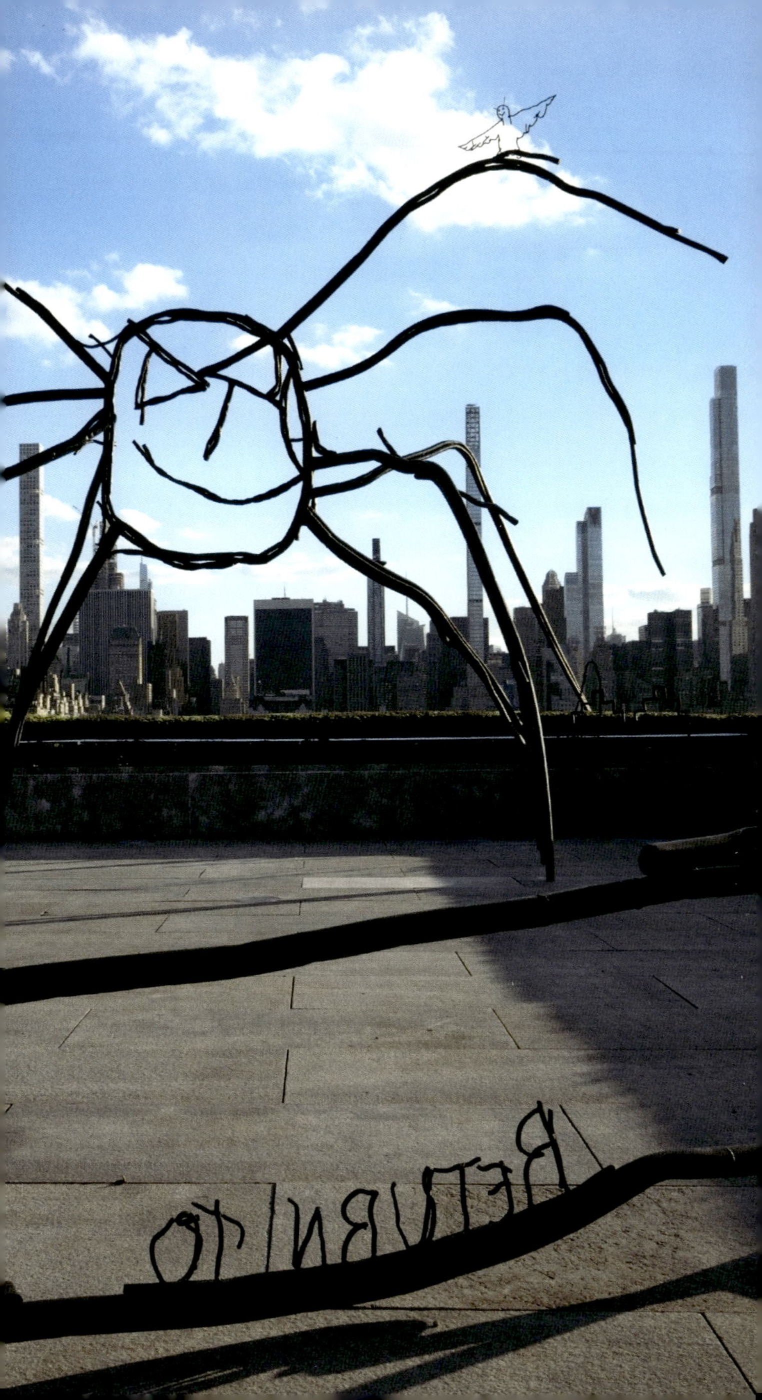
RETURN TO

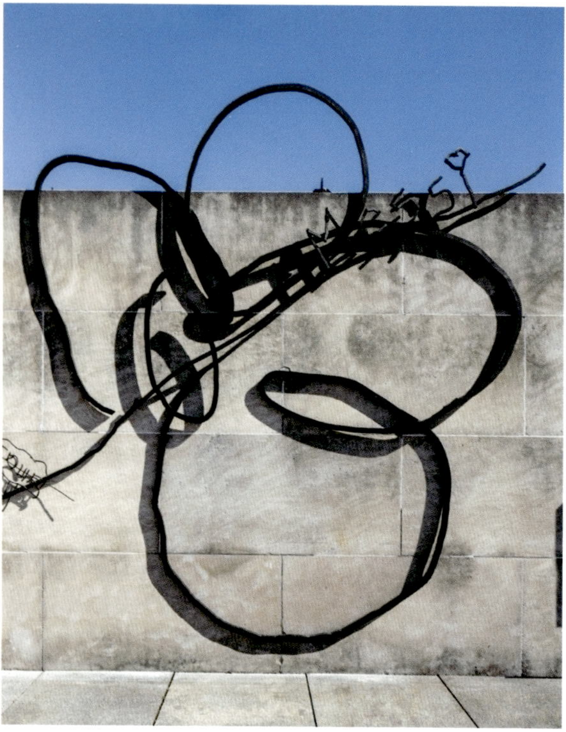

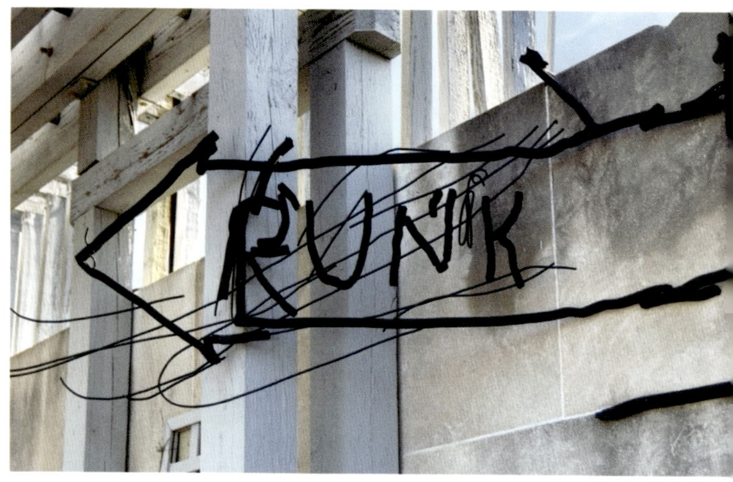
RUNK

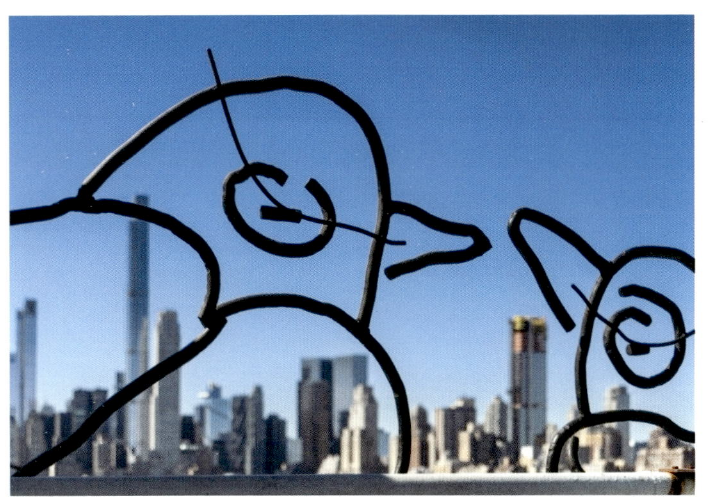

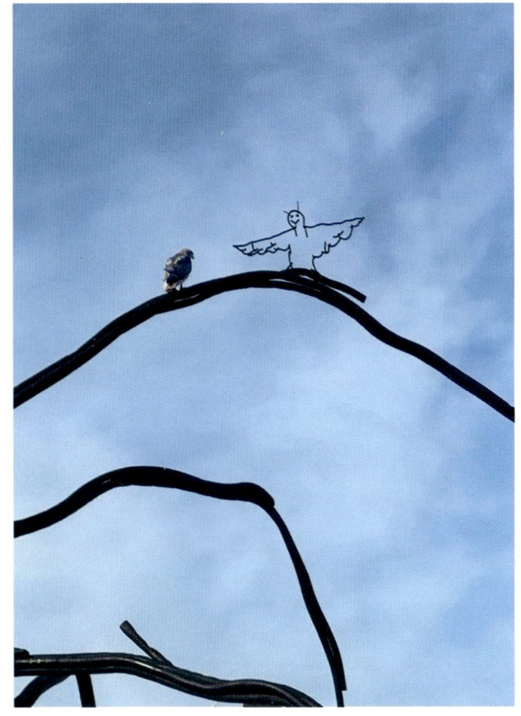

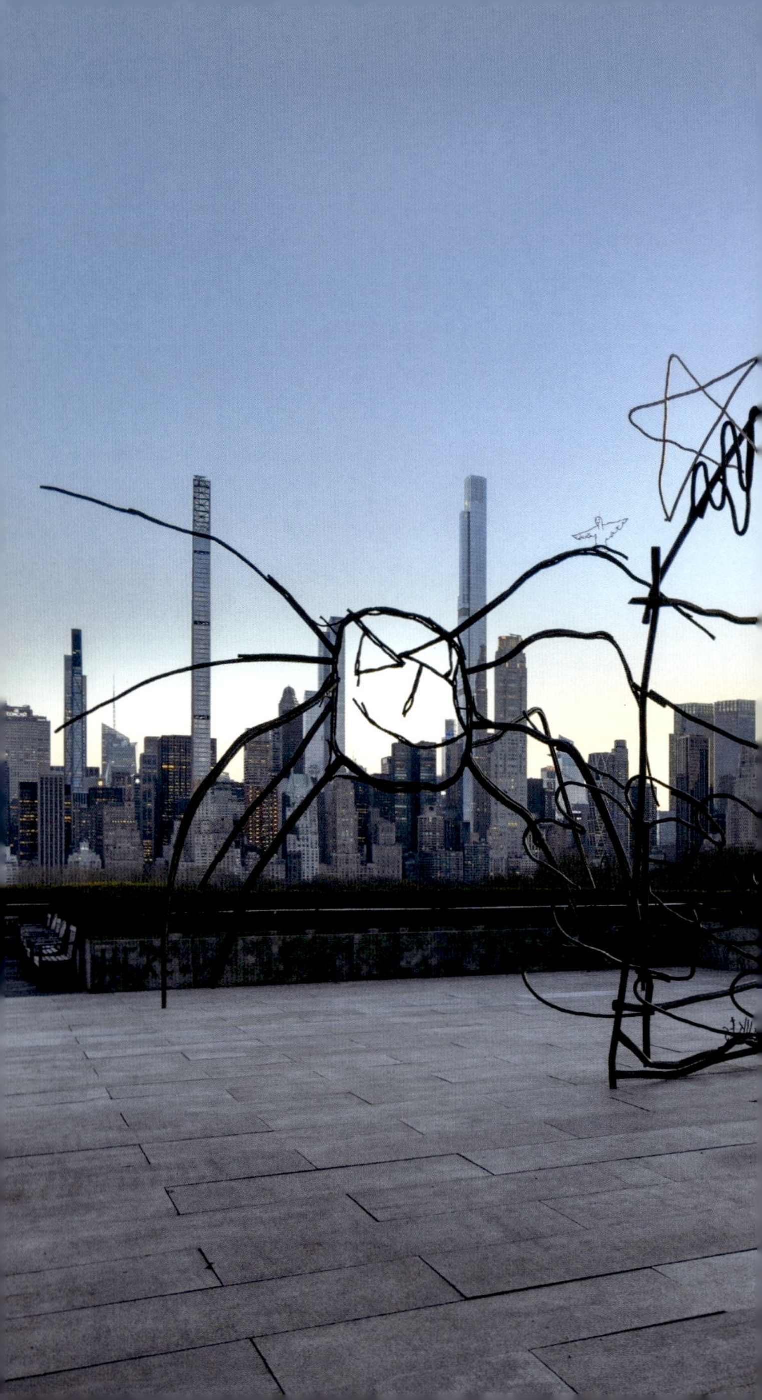

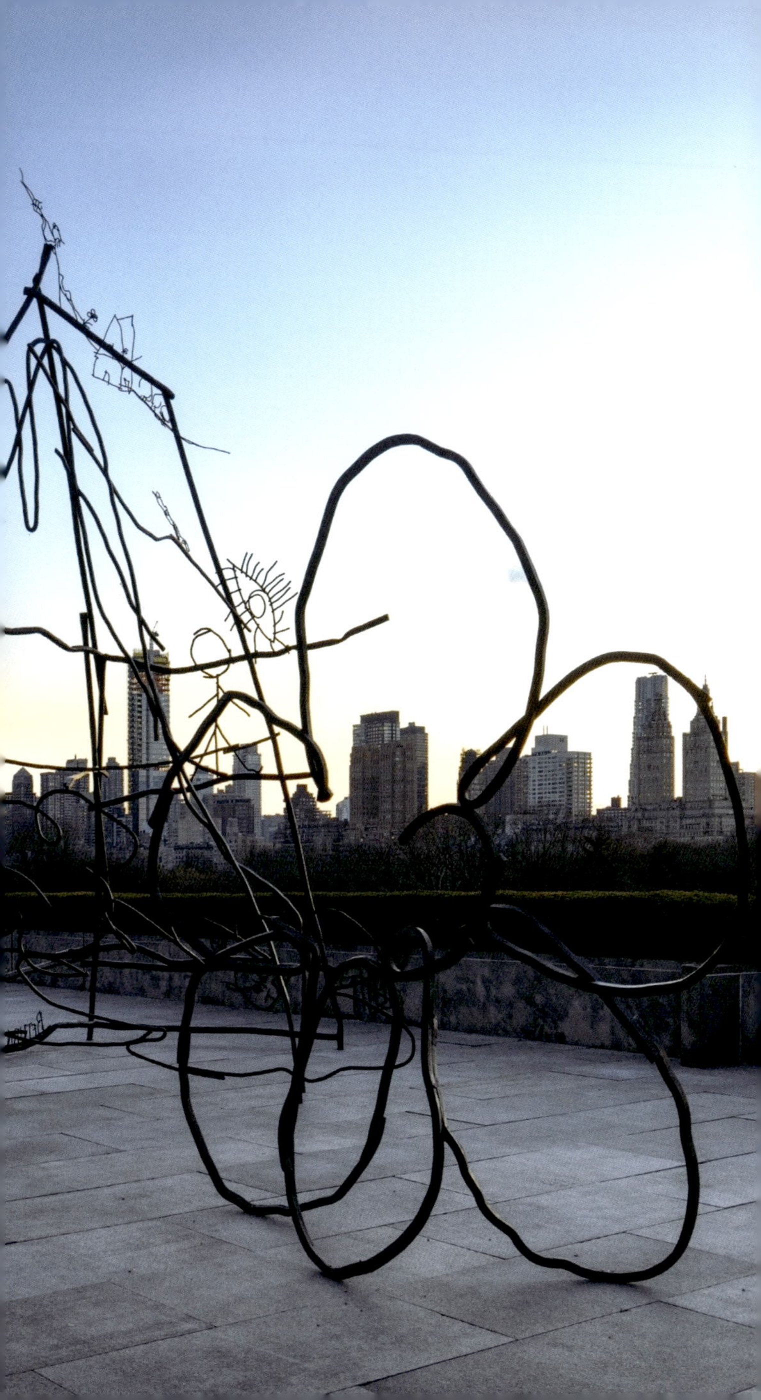

Selected Exhibition History

Solo Exhibitions

2023
Petrit Halilaj: RUNIK, Museo Tamayo, Mexico City

Very volcanic over this green feather, International Red Cross and Red Crescent Museum, Geneva

Lunar Ensemble for Uprising Seas (with Álvaro Urbano), in *Thus waves come in pairs,* TBA21–Academy's Ocean Space, Venice

2022
You used to fly, go everywhere and wake up those who are asleep, Fries Museum, Leeuwarden, Netherlands

2021
Very volcanic over this green feather, Tate St Ives, Cornwall, United Kingdom

2020
To a raven and hurricanes that from unknown places bring back smells of humans in love, Palacio de Cristal, Museo Nacional Centro de Arte Reina Sofía, Madrid

2018
Shkrepëtima, Runik, Kosovo; Zentrum Paul Klee, Bern; and Fondazione Merz, Turin (Mario Merz Prize)

Hammer Projects: Petrit Halilaj, Hammer Museum, Los Angeles

2017
RU, New Museum, New York

2015
Space Shuttle in the Garden, HangarBicocca, Milan

Abetare, Kölnischer Kunstverein, Cologne

She, fully turning around, became terrestrial, Kunst- und Ausstellungshalle der Bundesrepublik Deutschland, Bonn

2014
I'm hungry to keep you close. I want to find the words to resist but in the end there is a locked sphere. The funny thing is that you're not here, nothing is, Kunsthalle Lissabon

Darling squeeze the button and remove my memory, Galeria e Arteve e Kosovës, Pristina

2013
Poisoned by men in need of some love, WIELS Contemporary Art Centre, Brussels

Kosovo Pavilion, 55th Venice Bienniale

2012
Who does the earth belong to while painting the wind?!, Kunsthalle Sankt Gallen, Switzerland

2011
Petrit Halilaj, Kunstraum Innsbruck, Austria

2009
Petrit Halilaj: Back to the Future, Stacion - Center for Contemporary Art Prishtina

Selected Group Exhibitions

2023
NGV Triennial, Melbourne

2022
It matters what worlds world worlds: how to tell stories otherwise, Manifesta 14, Pristina, Kosovo

Evidence, Mercer Union, Toronto

2021
3rd Autostrada Biennale, National Library, Pristina, Kosovo

2020
FUORI, 17th Quadriennale d'Arte, Palazzo delle Esposizioni, Rome

2019
Where Water Comes Together with Other Water, 15th Lyon Biennale

2018
CHILDHOOD: Another banana day for the dream-fish, Palais de Tokyo, Paris

2017
Viva Arte Viva, 57th International Art Exhibition, Venice Biennale

2016
Shaping Ideas: Sculptures, Lewben Art Foundation, Vilnius

2015
Thirty One, National Gallery of Kosovo, Pristina

Slip of the Tongue, Palazzo Grassi—Punta della Dogana, Venice

2014
Shit and Die, Palazzo Cavour, Turin

Villa Romana-Preisträger 2014, Villa Romana, Florence

2012
30 Künstler/30 Räume, Kunstverein Nürnberg — Albrecht Dürer Gesellschaft

2011
Based in Berlin, Atelierhaus Monbijoupark, Berlin

2010
6th Berlin Biennale for Contemporary Art, KW Institute for Contemporary Art, Berlin

1999
Bambini di Kukës, Palazzo Municipale di Cremona, Italy

Annan, Kofi A., with Nader Mousavizadeh. *Interventions: A Life in War and Peace*. New York: Penguin Press, 2012.

Barlow, Anne, and Giles Jackson. *Petrit Halilaj: Very volcanic over this green feather*. Exh cat. St Ives, Cornwall, UK: Tate St Ives; London: Tate Publishing, 2021.

Casavecchia, Barbara. "Petrit Halilaj, *Poisoned by men in need of some love* at WIELS Contemporary Art Centre, Brussels." *Mousse* 40 (October–November 2013), pp. 166–69.

Casavecchia, Barbara, ed. *Thus Waves Come in Pairs: Thinking with the Mediterraneans*. London: Sternberg Press, 2023.

De Bellis, Vincenzo, and Alessandro Rabottini. *Strata: Italian Art since 2000: The Words of the Artists*. Milan: Lenz; Paris: Les presses du réel, 2023.

Donauer, Carla, and Susanne Kleine. *Petrit Halilaj*. Exh. cat. Cologne: Kölnischer Kunstverein and Verlag der Buchhandlung Walther König, 2015.

Filipovic, Elena, ed. *Petrit Halilaj: Poisoned by men in need of some love*. Exh. cat. Brussels: WIELS Contemporary Art Centre; Berlin: Motto Books, 2013.

Frith, Clifford B., and Dawn W. Frith. *The Bowerbirds*. New York: Oxford University Press, 2004.

Girardeau, Zérane S. *Déflagrations: Dessins d'enfants, guerres d'adultes*. Paris: Anamosa, 2017.

Godfrey, Mark. "Flight Fantasies." *Artforum* 60, no. 3 (November 2021), pp. 146–52.

Halilaj, Blerina, and Petrit Halilaj. "Communication seems to be lacking us as well." *Gagarin: The Artists in Their Own Words* 19. Gaga VZW: Antwerp: 2009.

Halilaj, Petrit. *Of course blue affects my way of shitting*. Berlin: Chert and Motto Books, 2014.

Malcolm, Noel. *Kosovo: A Short History*. London: Pan Books, 2002.

Scardi, Gabi, and Petrit Halilaj. "Storia di un abbraccio (fra specie)." *L'arte per l'altro, ancora (vol. 2): Animot* 11. Pordenone, Italy: Safarà Editore, 2021.

Statovci, Pajtim. *My Cat Yugoslavia*. New York: Pantheon, 2017.

Todorova, Maria. *Imagining the Balkans*. New York: Oxford University Press, 2009.

Trakilović, Miloš. "Petrit Halilaj: Portable Paradise." *Badland* 5 (2022).

Photography Credits

Acknowledgments

First and foremost, I would like to express my profound gratitude to Petrit Halilaj for accepting our invitation to produce this commission and for bringing such creative vision to this project. It has been a pleasure working with him, and I'm grateful for our inspiring conversations during these past years and for his generosity in allowing me to peek into his world.

Petrit has an amazing group of collaborators who contributed to every aspect of realizing this project. I'd like to recognize the invaluable assistance of his studio team, especially Serena Rota, Studio Manager, and Ferdinand Pechmann, Technical Manager. Vanina Saracino, Research Advisor, made important editorial contributions to this book.

At The Met, this commission would not have been possible without the support of Max Hollein, Marina Kellen French Director and CEO, and the advocacy of Sheena Wagstaff, former Leonard A. Lauder Chair, Department of Modern and Contemporary Art, who selected Petrit for this commission. David Breslin, Leonard A. Lauder Curator in Charge, Department of Modern and Contemporary Art, became a vital interlocutor throughout the evolution of the installation and contributed an insightful essay to this publication, for which I am most grateful.

The organization of the project has been adeptly managed and supported by various colleagues in the Museum, starting with Quincy Houghton, Deputy Director for Exhibitions and International Initiatives. Special recognition is due to Zoe Tippl, Senior Exhibitions Project Manager, whose tireless efforts have been indispensable in the success of the commission. I thank Katy Uravitch, Senior Manager, Administration, Operations, and Collection Management in the Department of Modern and Contemporary Art, for her support and guidance along the way. My gratitude extends to Marci King, Exhibitions Project Manager for Administration; Taylor Miller, Buildings Manager for Exhibitions; Allison Barone, Senior Associate Registrar; Amy Desmond Lamberti, Associate General Counsel; and Emily Balter, Assistant General Counsel. For their expert advice on materials, access, and safety, I am grateful to Kendra Roth, Objects Conservator; Deborah Gul Haffner, Environmental Health and Safety Manager; and Rebecca McGinnis, Mary Jaharis Senior Managing Educator, Accessibility. Thanks are also due to Harrison Carter, Graphic Designer, and the staff members in Digital who oversaw the production of the promo video: Melissa Bell, Kate Farrell, and Lela Jenkins. Other coworkers in the Department of Modern and Contemporary Art who provided invaluable assistance include Mallory Roark, Alejandro Leal Pulido, and Skye Prosper.

My colleagues in Development have been essential in securing the long-term sustainability and financial support that makes the Roof Garden commissions possible, and I'd like to extend my thanks to Whitney Donhauser, Jason Herrick, Hannah Howe, and John L. Wielk. In External Affairs, Alexandra Kozlakowski has been instrumental in presenting this visionary project to our public audiences.

This book is the result of a collaboration with key colleagues in The Met's Publications and Editorial Department. Jennifer Bantz was my thoughtful and patient editor, and Lauren Knighton deftly managed the book's production. Jenn Sherman sourced the images, Hyla Skopitz evocatively captured the atmosphere and presence of this commission, and Gina Rossi was responsible for the beautiful design. Mark Polizzotti, Michael Sittenfeld, and Peter Antony are due recognition for their continued dedication to the publication of these Roof Garden catalogues, which now, in their eleventh iteration, exist as a rather collectible set of volumes, documenting an important series of artist commissions at The Met.

Finally, my sincere thanks go to Bloomberg Philanthropies for its long-standing sponsorship of these commissions, to Cynthia Hazen Polsky and Leon B. Polsky for their steadfast support. My gratitude is also owed to the Diane W. and James E. Burke Fund and the Edward John & Patricia Rosenwald Foundation. The publication of this book has been made possible through the generosity of the Mary and Louis S. Myers Foundation Endowment Fund, for which I am grateful.

Iria Candela
Estrellita B. Brodsky Curator of Latin American Art
Department of Modern and Contemporary Art

The artist acknowledges the following for their work realizing this project:
Studio Petrit Halilaj: Serena Rota (studio manager), Ferdinand Pechmann (production manager), Hugo Larquè (workshop manager), Vanina Saracino (research), Rosario Moran and Christina Stathakopoulou (visualizations, 3D models), Veronica Paredes (accounting), Mirjam Khera (studio assistant), Martina Pelacchi (production); collaborators: Christina Werner (research advisor), Juan Echavarria, Mattia Bertolo, Toni Flügel, Anka Mirkin, Max Negrelli, Samuel von Düffel, Hagar Ophir, Nathan Stone, Joe Highton, and Fritz Rahne; Bernd Euler, Senta Hoppe, and the team at Euler GmbH, and Skulpturengießerei Knaak (artwork production); and Will Laufs and Kirill Kiselev (engineering); *Abetare* research in the Balkans: Amy Zion (research advisor), Leutrim Fishekqiu, Vatra Abrashi, Adrian Berisha, Arjon Kajtazi, Rrahim Dervishi, Hava Dako, Nikola Uzunovski, Olsi Lelaj, Amar Agić, Armin Ličina, Lushi Ismailaj, Valmira Morina, Lea Vene, Adela Železnik, Dzeni Rostohar, Zdenka Badovinac, Natalija Veselič Martinjak, Shaha Hyseni, Sofija Balać, Dzeni Rostohar, and Matej Jurčevoć.

The artist would like to thank his studio and The Met team, in particular Max Hollein, David Breslin, Iria Candela, Zoe Tippl, Katy Uravitch, Taylor Miller, and Allison Barone; Sheena Wagstaff and Pari Stave; his teachers, especially Sokol Uka, Rukmane Miftaraj, Behlul Spahiu, Eshref Qahili, Avni Curri, Alberto Garutti, Fabrizio Gazzarri, Laura Cherubini, Giacinto Di Pietrantonio, Drita Kadriu, and Murat Emini (in memory); his family and friends: Álvaro Urbano, Shkurte Halilaj, Gani Halilaj, Hana Halilaj, Blerina Halilaj, Blerim Halilaj, Driton Halilaj, Ardiana Halilaj, Alberta Doko Halilaj, Marina Begarelli, Giacomo Poli, Federica Poli, Tyra Tingleff, Moritz Wesseler, José Esparza Chong Cuy, and Sébastien Delot; the galleries' team: Jennifer Chert, Florian Lüdde, Clarissa Tempestini, Kamel Mennour, Emma Charlotte Gobry-Laurencin, Alexandra Khazina, Monica Manzutto, José Kuri, and Alexander Ferrando; and everyone else who collaborated on this project.

This catalogue is published in conjunction with *The Roof Garden Commission: Petrit Halilaj, Abetare* on view at The Metropolitan Museum of Art, New York, from April 30 through October 27, 2024.

The exhibition is supported by

Bloomberg Philanthropies

Additional support is provided by the Diane W. and James E. Burke Fund, Cynthia Hazen Polsky and Leon B. Polsky, and the Edward John & Patricia Rosenwald Foundation.

The catalogue is made possible by the Mary and Louis S. Myers Foundation Endowment Fund.

Published by The Metropolitan Museum of Art, New York

Mark Polizzotti, Publisher and Editor in Chief

Peter Antony, Associate Publisher for Production

Michael Sittenfeld, Associate Publisher for Editorial

Edited by Jennifer Bantz

Designed by Gina Rossi

Production by Lauren Knighton

Image acquisitions and permissions by Jenn Sherman

Photographs of works in The Met collection are by the Imaging Department, The Metropolitan Museum of Art, unless otherwise noted.

Additional photography credits appear on page 62.

Typeset in Galaxie Polaris and Chronicle

Printed on Endurance Silk 100lb

Separations by Professional Graphics, Inc., Rockford, Illinois

Printed and bound by GHP Media, Inc., West Haven, Connecticut

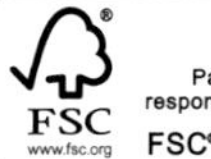

Front and back covers and pp. 1, 4, 6, 8, 53–59: *Abetare*, 2024. Photography by Hyla Skopitz

Page 2: Petrit Halilaj, 2021. Photography by Angela B Suarez

The Metropolitan Museum of Art endeavors to respect copyright in a manner consistent with its nonprofit educational mission. If you believe any material has been included in this publication improperly, please contact the Publications and Editorial Department.

The Metropolitan Museum of Art
1000 Fifth Avenue
New York, New York 10028
metmuseum.org

Distributed by
Yale University Press,
New Haven and London
yalebooks.com/art
yalebooks.co.uk

Cataloguing-in-Publication Data is available from the Library of Congress.

ISBN 978-1-58839-776-8